HAND IN HAND
WITH LOVE

An anthology of queer classic poetry

More poetry anthologies available from
Macmillan Collector's Library

Sunrise: Poems to Kick-Start Your Day ed. Susie Gibbs

My Heart's in the Highlands: Classic Scottish Poems
ed. Gaby Morgan

Poems about Birds ed. H. J. Massingham

Poems for New Parents ed. Becky Brown

Poems for Stillness introduced by Ana Sampson

Happy Hour: Poems to Raise a Glass to introduced by
Jancis Robinson

Poems of the Sea introduced by Adam Nicolson

Poems for Happiness introduced by Richard Coles

Poems for Travellers introduced by Paul Theroux

Poems for Christmas introduced by Judith Flanders

Poems of Childhood introduced by Michael Morpurgo

Poems on Nature introduced by Helen Macdonald

Poems for Love introduced by Joanna Trollope

The Golden Treasury ed. Francis Turner Palgrave

HAND IN HAND
WITH LOVE

An anthology of queer classic poetry

Edited and introduced by
SIMON AVERY

MACMILLAN COLLECTOR'S LIBRARY

This collection first published 2023 by Macmillan Collector's Library
an imprint of Pan Macmillan
The Smithson, 6 Briset Street, London EC1M 5NR
EU representative: Macmillan Publishers Ireland Ltd, 1st Floor,
The Liffey Trust Centre, 117–126 Sheriff Street Upper,
Dublin 1, DO1 YC43
Associated companies throughout the world
www.panmacmillan.com

ISBN 978-1-5290-9266-0

Selection, arrangement and introduction copyright © Simon Avery 2023

The Permissions Acknowledgements on p. 193 constitute an extension
of this copyright page.

1 3 5 7 9 8 6 4 2

A CIP catalogue record for this book is available from the British Library.

Casing design and endpaper pattern by Andrew Davidson
Typeset by Jouve (UK), Milton Keynes
Printed and bound in China by Imago

MIX
Paper | Supporting
responsible forestry
FSC® C116313
www.fsc.org

Visit **www.panmacmillan.com** to read more
about all our books and to buy them.

Contents

vi

EARLY TWENTIETH CENTURY

FURTHER DEVELOPMENTS

Introduction

SIMON AVERY

In May 1988, Margaret Thatcher's Tory government ushered in Section 28 of the Local Government Act, a divisive and damaging piece of legislation that made 'promotion' of homosexuality by local councils illegal. At a time when queer communities were already battling with a right-wing backlash and increased homophobia because of the AIDS crisis, Section 28 effectively closed down discussion of queer desire, experiences and identities. Teachers feared for their jobs if they talked about homosexuality with their students, public libraries were anxious about the books they made available and a general silencing descended on public discourse. Despite widespread protests against the Act by queer groups, Section 28 remained in place until 2000 in Scotland and 2003 in the rest of the UK.

I'm starting here because in many ways this attempt at silencing and the attendant right to a voice and acknowledgement have been – and remain – intricately bound up with queer cultures and politics. And silencing and voicing are repeatedly central to the poetry collected in this anthology. Probably the most famous phrase of queer poetry, 'the love that dare not speak its name', which is taken from Alfred Douglas's 'Two Loves' and which was quoted and interrogated at Oscar Wilde's second trial for 'acts of gross indecency' with other men in 1895, most clearly sums up this tension. Yet at the same time, Douglas has spent a longish poem purposely *bringing* a voice to queer desire and experiences, as do all the poets in this volume. The potential power of queer poetry is therefore vast, deploying wide varieties of language, imagery and form in order to assert difference, call for recognition and shape politics.

The term 'queer' itself has a diverse and shifting history. Its older and colloquial meaning links it to what is perceived as odd, strange and eccentric. My grandmother, born in 1908, used the word in this way to describe any number of things and events. However, across much of the twentieth century, 'queer' was also used as a derogatory term and a term of abuse to refer specifically to gay men. Then, in the late 1980s and early 1990s, 'queer' was reappropriated by political groups like ACT UP and Queer Nation as part of the political campaigns emerging in response to the AIDS crisis. And now, in the twenty-first century, it's often used as an umbrella term for LGBTQIA+ people, communities and identities (indicating lesbian, gay, bisexual, trans, queer, intersex and asexual, with that important '+' sign for other possibilities).

In this anthology, I use queer to indicate those desires, sexualities and identities that challenge and disrupt conventional categories and orthodoxies. The poems here reflect upon same-sex desires and experiences but also bisexuality, sexual independence, queer romantic 'friendship', eroticized religious and mystical experiences, queer landscapes and urbanscapes, queer histories, queer communities and possible queer utopias. The poems are drawn from the classical period to the present and I've chosen to present them chronologically, wherever possible, by date of publication. This isn't to suggest that being queer or writing about queer experiences always gets better or easier across the centuries – history is never that 'straight'-forward. But there are some fascinating developments and shifts and it's interesting to trace the continuities as well as the changes in the ways that poets write about sexuality, desire and queerness.

The oldest poetry included here is by the Ancient Greek poet Sappho, who is often cited as the originator of lyric poetry and whose work, mostly surviving only in fragments, is full of intense longing, sensuality and desire for women. The poem 'Passion', for example, intriguingly examines the relations between desire, the body and the mind, whilst 'Anagora' records Sappho's love for a priestess and 'The Garden of the Nymphs' has the speaker, half hidden, watching the nymphs binding their hair and touching each other's 'glisten[ing]' bodies. The beautiful landscape here, dreamlike and fecund, helps establish an important link between queerness and the pastoral – a space that is removed from the social world with all its attendant oppressions and conventions – which has subsequently become a frequent trope in queer literature across the centuries.

Significantly, however, most translations of Sappho's work until the late nineteenth century suppressed the expression of her love for other women, 're-gendering' the poems to make them 'safe'. This practice has much to tell us about the literary and social expression of female same-sex desire. Terry Castle has famously spoken of 'the apparitional lesbian', the title of her landmark critical study published in 1993, where she argues that the lesbian has often been invisible, marginalized or disembodied in modern culture. (It's interesting in this context to consider how many poems in this anthology depict queer desire using ghostly and spectral images.) And this 'invisibility' is certainly present in the history of women's poetry, where writers have often resorted to more covert ways of expressing queer desire because of social expectations. For example, many eighteenth-century women poets like Katherine Philips and Anna Seward wrote poems addressed to other women that purposely blur the lines between friendship, romance and sexual attraction. In 'To My Excellent Lucasia', Philips asserts that 'No bridegroom's nor crown-conqueror's mirth / To mine compared can be', whilst Seward, whose key relationships were all with women, wrote to Honora Sneyd of her 'loved form' and the fear of losing her affection. It was a bold woman like Aphra Behn who would write more overtly sexual work, speaking in 'The Dream' of the 'Rapture' of lying with Aminta, who knows 'the last Mystery of Love'. Interestingly, this framing of more challenging ideas and representations within a dream or vision is a technique used by other queer poets such as Alfred Douglas and Sarah Orne Jewett as a means of both revealing deep desires and possibly offsetting criticism for them ('it's just a dream').

Like all poets, writers of queer poetry are constantly searching for suitable forms to express their concerns. In the Renaissance, a number of male poets turned to the sonnet, subverting the form's roots in the expression of heterosexual love in order to speak of same-sex desire. Richard Barnfield, for instance, explores the anxieties of admitting his same-sex devotion in 'Sighing, and sadly sitting by my love', whilst unreservedly celebrating the male body though the traditional *blazon* technique (the listing of body parts) in 'Cherry-lipt Adonis'. Of Shakespeare's 154 sonnets published in 1609, 126 are addressed to a male 'Fair Youth' and include some of his most intricate writings on the value of love, the ability of love to survive change and the ways in which poetry can preserve the youth of the beloved. 'If this be error and upon me prov'd, / I never writ, nor no man ever lov'd' ends Sonnet 116 with a telling playfulness. And with the sonnet revival in the Romantic period, the form was again used in connection with queer subjects in works such as Keats' address 'To a Friend who sent me some roses', Wordsworth's sonnet to Eleanor Butler and Sarah Ponsby, the famous queer Ladies of Llangollen whom he terms 'Sisters in love', and Eliza Cook's sonnet to Charlotte Cushman, the American actress who lived in Rome in a 'Boston marriage' and with whom Cook is meant to have had an affair. These complexities are arguably taken even further in Elizabeth Barrett Browning's astonishing 'To George Sand: A Desire', where the traditional sonnet is subverted to celebrate the cross-dressing novelist Amantine Lucile Aurore Dupin, 'Thou large-brained woman and large-hearted man', in ways that link queerness with empowerment and radical writing. The tightness and intensity of the sonnet form consequently offered these and later writers an efficient means of framing their challenging views.

As the nineteenth century progressed, remarkable experimentation and a good degree of risk-taking occurred in poetic depictions of queer desires and relationships. Alfred Tennyson effectively queered the elegy in his long poem 'In Memoriam', where he details his grief for Arthur Hallam with incredible sensitivity, gender fluidity (he terms himself both widow and widower at points) and heart-wrenching images of loss (the alliterated monosyllables of the line 'On the bald street breaks the blank day' always gets me). Christina Rossetti's wonderfully seductive narrative poem, 'Goblin

Market', depicts the threat of male sexuality symbolized in the animalistic goblins hawking their fruit and suggests that resistance and empowerment lie in 'sisterly' same-sex desire. And in America, Walt Whitman's democratic celebration of unabashed bodies and sexualities in his extensive *Leaves of Grass*, alongside Emily Dickinson's compact, elliptical verses with their explorations of women's bodies and 'Wild Nights', effectively link queerness to the ongoing forging of the modern nation.

In the last decades of the nineteenth century, sexualities came to be discussed more widely in relation to shifting ideas about gender, women's rights and religion and the new insights emerging from psychology and sexology (the 'scientific' analysis of sexual behaviours). In these contexts, something of an explosion of queer writing occurred. The decadent poetry of Wilde, Douglas and Marc-André Raffalovich, for example, examines male same-sex desire from a variety of angles, including both shame and revelry, whilst Mary Coleridge and John Addington Symonds consider the possibilities of queer utopias associated with liberation and acceptance. Alternative desires are explored in the sadomasochism of Algernon Swinburne's poetry and the eroticized religious experience depicted by Mathilde Blind in 'The Mystic's Vision' (a connection that stretches back to the sexualized mysticism of Emily Brontë's 'The Prisoner' in the 1840s and John Donne's call to be ravished by God in 'Batter My Heart' in the early sixteenth century). And the radical aunt and niece, Katherine Bradley and Edith Cooper, who were both lovers and co-writers publishing under the pseudonym 'Michael Field', produced fascinating work focusing on the female body, sensual nature and classical mythology, asserting their resistance to convention through their creative and personal union: 'My Love and I took hands and swore, / Against the world, to be / Poets and lovers evermore' ('It was deep April').

The excitement and variety of queer work in the fin de siècle, as well as the reworking of now established tropes such as the ghost of repressed or marginalized desire, queer pastoral, the dream or vision and the emphasis on bodily touch, were subsequently taken further in the new socio-political contexts of the early twentieth century. The long shadow of the 1895 Wilde trials can be felt in many poems of anxiety and unspoken love, as well as in the sharp critiques of law in A. E. Housman's poems and the call for a safe community in Edna St Vincent Millay's 'Tavern'. These anxieties were exacerbated by the devastating impact of the First World War, which radically changed the ways poets such as Sydney Oswald, W. N. Hodgson and Wilfred Owen reflected upon the male youth, structures of loss and the eroticized (dead) body, as well as inspiring some especially reflective poems about queer ageing by Rupert Brooke, Amy Lowell and Claude McKay. And in post-war America, the queer poets of the Harlem Renaissance, McKay and Countee Cullen, opened up new and urgent questions about the complex intersections between sexuality, race and class, many of which still demand attention. As ever, queer poetry is intricately bound up with change and modernity.

The title of this volume, *Hand in Hand with Love*, comes from Wilde's beautiful poem 'Apologia', which argues that it's better to have lived life, as difficult as it might be, than let opportunities go by. The phrasing gestures towards both the idea of companionship and all those experiences and emotions that are bound up with relationships (that come 'hand in hand' with them). When I started putting this anthology together, I had an initial sense of poems I'd like to include to show this and some of the ideas I wanted to focus on. But as I read more, I became astonished by the sheer variety, quantity and power of the queer poems I was coming across, and intrigued by the multiple and ever-expanding ways in which poets address queer experiences. From the bawdiness of Catullus and the tenderness of Christopher Marlowe, through to the unsettling gothic of Charlotte Mew and the relatively forgotten erotics of Australian poet Lesbia Harford, these poems reveal how similar concerns resurface and modulate across different time periods and in different socio-political contexts.

The power of language and imagery in this body of work is constantly re-energized, and forms such as the lyric, the sonnet and the narrative poem are themselves rewritten and queered. Indeed, the final section here, 'Further Developments', clearly demonstrates how queer poetry continues to change and address pressing issues. Here, the writings of Audre Lorde, Thom Gunn, Roz Kaveney and Travis Alabanza foreground the position of marginalized groups ('those of us who live at the shoreline', as Lorde puts it), interrogate queer histories (the Stonewall Riots and the AIDS crisis) and reclaim positions of power ('you cannot fuck with me', asserts Alabanza at the close of 'Pride'). Throughout the two and a half millennia represented in this anthology, it's both this aesthetic skill and the political power of the work – power to challenge hierarchies, to resist oppression and to demand we look at the world differently – that make queer poetry continually dynamic and provocative.

★

There are a number of people I'd like to thank for help with this project. Marissa Constantinou at Pan Macmillan has been incredibly supportive, insightful and patient throughout and a pleasure to work with. Kate M. Graham, Victoria Brookes, Lucy Bond, Peter Moore, Vicky Griffin, Matt Morrison, Alex Warwick, Helen Glew and Monica Germanà have all been willing to listen and advise as I've brought the material together and I'm hugely thankful for their ideas. The final work is dedicated to my wonderful partner, Tom Moore, who brings endless joy and delight into my world, 'hand in hand with love'.

HAND IN HAND
WITH LOVE

CLASSICAL

Passion

Now Love shakes my soul, a mighty
　　Wind from the high mountain falling
　　Full on the oaks of the forest;

Now, limb-relaxing, it masters
　　My life and implacable thrills me,
　　Rending with anguish and rapture.

Now my heart, paining my bosom,
　　Pants with desire as a mænad
　　Mad for the orgiac revel.

Now under my skin run subtle
　　Arrows of flame, and my body
　　Quivers with surge of emotion.

Now long importunate yearnings
　　Vanquish with surfeit my reason;
　　Fainting my senses forsake me.

Sappho (c. 630–570 BCE)
tr. John Myers O'Hara (1870–1944)

The Garden of the Nymphs

All around through the apple boughs in blossom
Murmur cool the breezes of early summer,
And from leaves that quiver above me gently
        Slumber is shaken;

Glades of poppies swoon in the drowsy languor,
Dreaming roses bend, and the oleanders
Bask and nod to drone of bees in the silent
        Fervor of noontide;

Myrtle coverts hedging the open vista,
Dear to nightly frolic of Nymph and Satyr,
Yield a mossy bed for the brown and weary
        Limbs of the shepherd.

Echo ever wafts through the drooping frondage,
Ceaseless silver murmur of water falling
In the grotto cool of the Nymphs, the sacred
        Haunt of Immortals;

Down the sides of rocks that are gray and lichened
Trickle tiny rills, whose expectant tinkle
Drips with gurgle hushed in the clear glimmering
        Depths of the basin.

Fair on royal couches of leaves recumbent,
Interspersed with languor of waxen lilies,
Lotus flowers empurple the pool whose edge is
        Cushioned with mosses;

Here recline the Nymphs at the hour of twilight,
Back in shadows dim of the cave, their golden
Sea-green eyes half lidded, up to their supple
       Waists in the water.

Sheltered once by ferns I espied them binding
Tresses long, the tint of lilac and orange;
Just beyond the shimmer of light their bodies
       Roseate glistened;

Deftly, then, they girdled their loins with garlands,
Linked with leaves luxuriant limb and shoulder;
On their breasts they bruised the red blood of roses
       Fresh from the garden.

She of orange hair was the Nymph Euxanthis,
And the lilac-tressed were Iphis and Io;
How they laughed, relating at length their ease in
       Evading the Satyr.

Sappho (c. 630–570 BCE)
tr. John Myers O'Hara (1870–1944)

The Stricken Flower

Think not to ever look as once of yore,
Atthis, upon my love; for thou no more
Wilt find intact upon its stem the flower
Thy guile left slain and bleeding in that hour.

So ruthless shepherds crush beneath their feet
The hill flower blooming in the summer heat;
The hyacinth whose purple heart is found
Left bruised and dead, to darken on the ground.

Sappho (c. 630–570 BCE)
tr. John Myers O'Hara (1870–1944)

Anagora

Anagora, fairest
Spoil of fateful battle,
Babylonian temples
Knew thy luring song.

Wrested from barbaric
Captors for thy beauty,
Thou wert made a priestess
At Mylitta's shrine.

Once these flexile fingers
Clasped in mine so closely,
Neath the temple's arches
Thrummed the tabor soft.

Thou hast taught me secrets
Of the cryptic chambers,
How the zonahs worship
In the burning East;

Raptures that my wildest
Dreaming never pictured,
Arts of love that charmed me,
Subtle, new and strange.

Hearken to my earnest
Prayer, O Aphrodite!
May the night be doubled
Now for our delight.

Sappho (c. 630–570 BCE)
tr. John Myers O'Hara (1870–1944)

Idyll XII

Art come, dear youth? two days and nights away!
(Who burn with love, grow aged in a day.)
As much as apples sweet the damson crude
Excel; the blooming spring the winter rude;
In fleece the sheep her lamb; the maid in sweetness
The thrice-wed dame; the fawn the calf in fleetness;
The nightingale in song all feathered kind—
So much thy longed-for presence cheers my mind.
To thee I hasten, as to shady beech,
The traveller, when from the heaven's reach
The sun fierce blazes. May our love be strong,
To all hereafter times the theme of song!
'Two men each other loved to that degree,
That either friend did in the other see
A dearer than himself. They lived of old
Both golden natures in an age of gold.'

O father Zeus! ageless immortals all!
Two hundred ages hence may one recall,
Down-coming to the irremeable river,
This to my mind, and this good news deliver:
'E'en now from east to west, from north to south,
Your mutual friendship lives in every mouth.'
This, as they please, th' Olympians will decide:
Of thee, by blooming virtue beautified,
My glowing song shall only truth disclose;
With falsehood's pustules I'll not shame my nose.
If thou dost sometime grieve me, sweet the pleasure
Of reconcilement, joy in double measure

To find thou never didst intend the pain,
And feel myself from all doubt free again.

Theocritus (c. 300–260 BCE)
tr. M. J. Chapman (c. 1836)

Long at our leisure yesterday

To Licinius

Long at our leisure yesterday
Idling, Licinius, we wrote
Upon my tablets verses gay,
Or took our turns, as fancy smote,
At rhymes and dice and wine.
   But when I left, Licinius mine,
Your grace and your facetious mood
Had fired me so, that neither food
Would stay my misery, nor sleep
My roving eyes in quiet keep.
But still consumed, without respite,
I tossed about my couch in vain
And longed for day—if speak I might,
Or be with you again.
   But when my limbs with all the strain
Worn out, half dead lay on my bed,
Sweet friend to thee this verse I penned,
That so thou mayest condescend
To understand my pain.
   So now, Licinius, beware!
And be not rash, but to my prayer
A gracious hearing tender;
Lest on thy head pounce Nemesis:
A goddess sudden and swift she is—
Beware lest thou offend her!

Catullus (c. 84–54 BCE)
tr. M. J. Chapman (c. 1836)

To Aurelius—Hands off the Boy!

To thee I trust my loves and me,
(Aurelius!) craving modesty.
That (if in mind didst ever long
To win aught chaste unknowing wrong)
Then guard my boy in purest way.
From folk I say not: naught affray
The crowds wont here and there to run
Through street-squares, busied every one;
But thee I dread nor less thy penis
Fair or foul, younglings' foe I ween is!
Wag it as wish thou, at its will,
When out of doors its hope fulfil;
Him bar I, modestly, methinks.
But should ill-mind or lust's high jinks
Thee (Sinner!), drive to sin so dread,
That durst ensnare our dearling's head,
Ah! woe's thee (wretch!) and evil fate,
Mullet and radish shall pierce and grate,
When feet-bound, haled through yawning gate.

Catullus (c. 84–54 BCE)
tr. Richard Burton (1821–1890)

RENAISSANCE & EIGHTEENTH CENTURY

My True Love Hath My Heart

My true love hath my heart and I have his,
By just exchange one for the other given:
I hold his dear, and mine he cannot miss;
There never was a bargain better driven.
His heart in me keeps me and him in one;
My heart in him his thoughts and senses guides:
He loves my heart, for once it was his own;
I cherish his because in me it bides.
His heart his wound received from my sight;
My heart was wounded with his wounded heart;
For as from me on him his hurt did light,
So still, methought, in me his hurt did smart:
Both equal hurt, in this change sought our bliss,
My true love hath my heart and I have his.

Philip Sidney (1554–1586)

Sighing, and sadly sitting by my love

Sighing, and sadly sitting by my love,
   He askt the cause of my hearts sorrowing,
   Conjuring me by heavens eternall King,
To tell the cause which me so much did move.
Compell'd: (quoth I) to thee will I confesse,
   Love is the cause; and only love it is
   That doth deprive me of my heavenly blisse,
Love is the paine that doth my heart oppresse.
And what is she (quoth he) who thou dos't love?
   Looke in this glasse (quoth I) there shalt thou see
   The perfect forme of my felicitie.
When, thinking that it would strange Magic prove,
   He open'd it: and taking off the cover
   He straight perceav'd himselfe to be my Lover.

Richard Barnfield (1574–1620)

16

Cherry-lipt Adonis in his snowie shape

Cherry-lipt Adonis in his snowie shape,
  Might not compare with his pure Ivorie white,
  On whose faire front a Poets pen may write,
Whose rosiate red excels the crimson grape,
His love-enticing delicate soft limbs,
  Are rarely fram'd t' intrap poore gazing eyes:
  His cheekes, the Lillie and Carnation dies,
With lovely tincture which Apollo's dims.
His lips ripe strawberries in Nectar wet,
  His mouth a Hive, his tongue a hony-combe,
  Where Muses (like Bees) make their mansion.
His teeth pure Pearle in blushing Correll set.
  Oh how can such a body sinne-procuring,
  Be slow to love, and quicke to hate, enduring?

Richard Barnfield (1574–1620)

The Passionate Shepherd to His Love

Come live with me and be my love,
And we will all the pleasures prove
That valleys, groves, hills, and fields,
Woods, or steepy mountain yields.

And we will sit upon the rocks,
Seeing the shepherds feed their flocks,
By shallow rivers to whose falls
Melodious birds sing madrigals.

And I will make thee beds of roses
And a thousand fragrant posies,
A cap of flowers, and a kirtle
Embroidered all with leaves of myrtle;

A gown made of the finest wool
Which from our pretty lambs we pull;
Fair lined slippers for the cold,
With buckles of the purest gold;

A belt of straw and ivy buds,
With coral clasps and amber studs:
And if these pleasures may thee move,
Come live with me, and be my love.

The shepherds' swains shall dance and sing
For thy delight each May morning:
If these delights thy mind may move,
Then live with me and be my love.

Christopher Marlowe (1564–1593)

When, in disgrace with fortune and men's eyes

When, in disgrace with fortune and men's eyes,
I all alone beweep my outcast state,
And trouble deaf heaven with my bootless cries,
And look upon myself and curse my fate,
Wishing me like to one more rich in hope,
Featur'd like him, like him with friends possess'd,
Desiring this man's art and that man's scope,
With what I most enjoy contented least;
Yet in these thoughts myself almost despising,
Haply I think on thee, and then my state,
Like to the lark at break of day arising
From sullen earth, sings hymns at heaven's gate;
  For thy sweet love remember'd such wealth
    brings
  That then I scorn to change my state with
    kings.

William Shakespeare (1564–1616)

Not marble nor the gilded monuments

Not marble nor the gilded monuments
Of princes shall outlive this powerful rhyme,
But you shall shine more bright in these contents
Than unswept stone besmeared with sluttish time.
When wasteful war shall statues overturn,
And broils root out the work of masonry,
Nor Mars his sword nor war's quick fire shall burn
The living record of your memory.
'Gainst death and all-oblivious enmity
Shall you pace forth; your praise shall still find room
Even in the eyes of all posterity
That wear this world out to the ending doom.
  So, till the Judgement that yourself arise,
  You live in this, and dwell in lovers' eyes.

William Shakespeare (1564–1616)

Let me not to the marriage of true minds

Let me not to the marriage of true minds
Admit impediments. Love is not love
Which alters when it alteration finds,
Or bends with the remover to remove.
O, no! it is an ever-fixed mark
That looks on tempests and is never shaken;
It is the star to every wandering bark,
Whose worth's unknown, although his height be
    taken.
Love's not Time's fool, though rosy lips and cheeks
Within his bending sickle's compass come;
Love alters not with his brief hours and weeks,
But bears it out even to the edge of doom.
  If this be error and upon me prov'd,
  I never writ, nor no man ever lov'd.

William Shakespeare (1564–1616)

The Anniversary

All kings, and all their favourites,
    All glory of honours, beauties, wits,
The sun itself, which makes time, as they pass,
Is elder by a year now than it was
When thou and I first one another saw.
All other things to their destruction draw,
    Only our love hath no decay;
This no to-morrow hath, nor yesterday;
Running it never runs from us away,
But truly keeps his first, last, everlasting day.

    Two graves must hide thine and my corse;
    If one might, death were no divorce.
Alas! as well as other princes, we
—Who prince enough in one another be—
Must leave at last in death these eyes and ears,
Oft fed with true oaths, and with sweet salt tears;
    But souls where nothing dwells but love
—All other thoughts being inmates—then shall prove
This or a love increasèd there above,
When bodies to their graves, souls from their graves
      remove.

    And then we shall be throughly blest;
    But now no more than all the rest.
Here upon earth we're kings, and none but we
Can be such kings, nor of such subjects be.

Who is so safe as we? where none can do
Treason to us, except one of us two.
   True and false fears let us refrain,
Let us love nobly, and live, and add again
Years and years unto years, till we attain
To write threescore; this is the second of our reign.

John Donne (1572–1631)

Batter my heart, three-person'd God

Batter my heart, three-person'd God, for you
As yet but knock, breathe, shine, and seek to mend;
That I may rise, and stand, o'erthrow me, and bend
Your force to break, blow, burn, and make me new.
I, like an usurped town, to another due,
Labour to admit you, but Oh, to no end.
Reason, your viceroy in me, me should defend,
But is captived, and proves weak or untrue.
Yet dearly I love you, and would be loved fain,
But am betrothed unto your enemy:
Divorce me, untie or break that knot again,
Take me to you, imprison me, for I,
Except you enthrall me, never shall be free,
Nor ever chaste, except you ravish me.

John Donne (1572–1631)

To My Excellent Lucasia, on Our Friendship

I did not live until this time
   Crowned my felicity,
When I could say without a crime,
   I am not thine, but thee.

This carcass breathed, and walked, and slept,
   So that the world believed
There was a soul the motions kept;
   But they were all deceived.

For as a watch by art is wound
   To motion, such was mine:
But never had Orinda found
   A soul till she found thine;

Which now inspires, cures and supplies,
   And guides my darkened breast:
For thou art all that I can prize,
   My joy, my life, my rest.

No bridegroom's nor crown-conqueror's mirth
   To mine compared can be:
They have but pieces of the earth,
   I've all the world in thee.

Then let our flames still light and shine,
   And no false fear control,
As innocent as our design,
   Immortal as our soul.

Katherine Philips (1632–1664)

The Dream

All trembling in my Arms Aminta lay,
Defending of the Bliss I strove to take;
Raising my Rapture by her kind delay,
Her force so charming was and weak.
The soft resistance did betray the Grant,
While I pressed on the Heaven of my desires;
Her rising Breasts with nimbler Motions Pant;
Her dying Eyes assume new Fires.
Now to the height of languishment she grows,
And still her looks new Charms put on;
Now the last Mystery of Love she knows,
We Sigh, and Kiss: I wak'd, and all was done.

'Twas but a Dream, yet by my Heart I knew,
Which still was Panting, part of it was true:
Oh how I strove the rest to have believ'd;
Asham'd and Angry to be undeceived!

Aphra Behn (1640–1689)

To the Fair Clorinda

WHO MADE LOVE TO ME,
IMAGIN'D MORE THAN WOMAN

Fair lovely Maid, or if that Title be
Too weak, too Feminine for Nobler thee,
Permit a Name that more Approaches Truth:
And let me call thee, Lovely Charming Youth.
This last will justifie my soft complainte,
While that may serve to lessen my constraint;
And without Blushes I the Youth persue,
When so much beauteous Woman is in view
Against thy Charms we struggle but in vain
With thy deluding Form thou giv'st us pain,
While the bright Nymph betrays us to the Swain.
In pity to our Sex sure thou wer't sent,
That we might Love, and yet be Innocent:
For sure no Crime with thee we can commit;
Or if we shou'd – thy Form excuses it.
For who, that gathers fairest Flowers believes
A Snake lies hid beneath the Fragrant Leaves.

Thou beauteous Wonder of a different kind,
Soft Cloris with the dear Alexis join'd;
When e'er the Manly part of thee, wou'd plead
Thou tempts us with the Image of the Maid,
While we the noblest Passions do extend
The Love to Hermes, Aphrodite the Friend.

Aphra Behn (1640–1689)

To Honora Sneyd

Honora, should that cruel time arrive
When 'gainst my truth thou should'st my errors poise,
Scorning remembrance of our vanished joys;
When for the love-warm looks in which I live,
But cold respect must greet me, that shall give
No tender glance, no kind regretful sighs;
When thou shalt pass me with averted eyes,
Feigning thou see'st me not, to sting, and grieve,
And sicken my sad heart, I could not bear
Such dire eclipse of thy soul-cheering rays;
I could not learn my struggling heart to tear
From thy loved form, that through my memory strays;
Nor in the pale horizon of Despair
Endure the wintry and the darkened days.

Anna Seward (1742–1809)

NINETEENTH CENTURY

To a Friend who sent me some Roses

As late I rambled in the happy fields,
   What time the sky-lark shakes the tremulous dew
   From his lush clover covert;—when anew
Adventurous knights take up their dinted shields:
I saw the sweetest flower wild nature yields,
   A fresh-blown musk-rose; 'twas the first that threw
   Its sweets upon the summer: graceful it grew
As is the wand that queen Titania wields.
And, as I feasted on its fragrancy,
   I thought the garden-rose it far excell'd:
But when, O Wells! thy roses came to me
   My sense with their deliciousness was spell'd:
Soft voices had they, that with tender plea
   Whisper'd of peace, and truth, and friendliness
     unquell'd.

John Keats (1795–1821)

To the Lady Eleanor Butler and
the Hon. Miss Ponsonby

*Composed in the Grounds of Plas Newydd,
near Llangollen, 1824*

A stream, to mingle with your favorite Dee,
Along the Vale of Meditation flows;
So styled by those fierce Britons, pleased to see
In Nature's face the expression of repose;
Or haply there some pious hermit chose
To live and die, the peace of heaven his aim;
To whom the wild, sequestered region owes,
At this late day, its sanctifying name,
Glyn Cafaillgaroch, in the Cambrian tongue,
In ours, the Vale of Friendship, let this spot
Be named; where, faithful to a low-roofed cot,
On Deva's banks ye have abode so long;
Sisters in love, a love allowed to climb,
Even on this earth, above the reach of time!

William Wordsworth (1770–1850)

Love and Death

1

I watched thee when the foe was at our side,
Ready to strike at him—or thee and me,
Were safety hopeless—rather than divide
Aught with one loved save love and liberty.

2

I watched thee on the breakers, when the rock
Received our prow, and all was storm and fear,
And bade thee cling to me through every shock;
This arm would be thy bark, or breast thy bier.

3

I watched thee when the fever glazed thine eyes,
Yielding my couch and stretched me on the ground
When overworn with watching, ne'er to rise
From thence if thou an early grave hadst found.

4

The earthquake came, and rocked the quivering wall,
And men and nature reeled as if with wine.
Whom did I seek around the tottering hall?
For thee. Whose safety first provide for? Thine.

And when convulsive throes denied my breath
The faintest utterance to my fading thought,
To thee—to thee—e'en in the gasp of death
My spirit turned, oh! oftener than it ought.

Thus much and more; and yet thou lov'st me not,
And never wilt! Love dwells not in our will.
Nor can I blame thee, though it be my lot
To strongly, wrongly, vainly love thee still.

George, Lord Byron (1788–1824)

A Young Girl Seen in Church

Was she an orphan?—can another grief
  So wholly chasten?—can another woe
So sanctify?—for she was (as a leaf
  Of hue funereal mid the Spring's young glow)
Robed in emphatic black:—the soul of night
  Filled her rich simply-parted ebon hair,
And raven eye-lashes, and made her bright
  With solemn lustre day can never wear.

Two younger buds, a sister at each side,
  Like little moon-lit clouds beside the moon,
Which up the sky's majestic temple glide,
  Clad darkly too, she led,—but music soon
Moved over her, and like a breeze of heaven,
  Shook from her lips the fragrance of her soul,—
And then, the thoughts with which my heart had
    striven,
  Spoke in my gaze, and would not brook control.

I bent upon her my astonished eye,
  That glowed, I felt, with an expression full
Of all that love which dares to deify,—
  That adoration of the beautiful
Which haunts the poet,—I forgot the sighs
  Of whispered prayer around me, and the page
Of hope divine, and the eternal eyes
  That look through every heart, in every place and
    age.
I gazed and gazed as though she were a star,
Unconscious and unfallen, which shone above, afar.—

But eloquently grave, a crimson cloud
    Of deep disquietude her cheek o'erspread
With exquisite rebuke;—and then I bowed
    Like hers my earnest looks and conscious head,
Ashamed to have disturbed the current meek
    Of her translucent thoughts, and made them flow
Painfully earthward. But she veiled that cheek,—
    Veiled even its sweet reproach and sacred glow,
Like those pure flowers too sensitive to brook
    Noon's burning eye, and its oppressive look,
That shut, in beautiful displeasure, up
    Each brilliant petal of their heart's deep cup.

Eliza Mary Hamilton (1807–1851)

To George Sand: A Desire

Thou large-brained woman and large-hearted man,
Self-called George Sand! whose soul, amid the lions
Of thy tumultuous senses, moans defiance
And answers roar for roar, as spirits can:
I would some mild miraculous thunder ran
Above the applauded circus, in appliance
Of thine own nobler nature's strength and science,
Drawing two pinions, white as wings of swan,
From thy strong shoulders, to amaze the place
With holier light! that thou to woman's claim
And man's, mightst join beside the angel's grace
Of a pure genius sanctified from blame
Till child and maiden pressed to thine embrace
To kiss upon thy lips a stainless fame.

Elizabeth Barrett Browning (1806–1861)

To Charlotte Cushman

*On Seeing Her Play 'Bianca' in Milman's
Tragedy of 'Fazio'*

I thought thee wondrous when thy soul portrayed
The youth Verona bragged of; and the love
Of glowing, southern blood by thee was made
Entrancing as the breath of orange-grove.

I felt the spirit of the great was thine:
In the fond Boy's devotion and despair;
I knew thou wert a pilgrim at the shrine
Where GOD's high ministers alone repair.

No rote-learned sighing filled thy doting moans;
Thy grief was heavy as thy joy was light;
Passion and Poesy were in thy tones,
And MIND flashed forth in its electric might.

I had seen many 'fret and strut their hour';
But my brain never had become such slave
To Fiction, as it did beneath thy power;
Nor owned such homage as to thee it gave.

I did not think thou couldst arouse a throb
Of deeper, stronger beating in my heart;
I did not deem thou couldst awake the sob
Of choking fulness, and convulsive start.

But thy pale madness, and thy gasping woe,
That breathed the torture of Bianca's pain;
Oh! never would my bosom ask to know
Such sad and bitter sympathy again!

When the wife's anguish sears thy hopeless cheek,
Let crowds behold and laud thee as they will;
But this poor breast, in shunning what they seek,
May yield, perchance, a richer tribute still.

Eliza Cook (1818–1889)

The Night-Wind

In summer's mellow midnight,
   A cloudless moon shone through
Our open parlour window,
   And rose-trees wet with dew.

I sat in silent musing;
   The soft wind waved my hair;
It told me heaven was glorious,
   And sleeping earth was fair.

I needed not its breathing
   To bring such thoughts to me;
But still it whispered lowly,
   How dark the woods will be!

'The thick leaves in my murmur
   Are rustling like a dream,
And all their myriad voices
   Instinct with spirit seem.'

I said, 'Go, gentle singer,
   Thy wooing voice is kind:
But do not think its music
   Has power to reach my mind.

'Play with the scented flower,
   The young tree's supple bough,
And leave my human feelings
   In their own course to flow.'

The wanderer would not heed me;
　　Its kiss grew warmer still.
'O come!' it sighed so sweetly;
　　'I'll win thee 'gainst thy will.

'Were we not friends from childhood?
　　Have I not loved thee long?
As long as thou, the solemn night,
　　Whose silence wakes my song.

'And when thy heart is resting
　　Beneath the church-aisle stone,
I shall have time for mourning,
　　And *thou* for being alone.'

Emily Brontë (1818–1848)

from The Prisoner

A messenger of Hope, comes every night to me,
And offers for short life, eternal liberty.

He comes with western winds, with evening's
    wandering airs,
With that clear dusk of heaven that brings the thickest
    stars.
Winds take a pensive tone, and stars a tender fire,
And visions rise, and change, that kill me with desire.

Desire for nothing known in my maturer years,
When Joy grew mad with awe, at counting future
    tears.
When, if my spirit's sky was full of flashes warm,
I knew not whence they came, from sun, or thunder
    storm.

But, first, a hush of peace—a soundless calm
    descends;
The struggle of distress, and fierce impatience ends.
Mute music soothes my breast, unuttered harmony,
That I could never dream, till Earth was lost to me.

Then dawns the Invisible; the Unseen its truth
    reveals;
My outward sense is gone, my inward essence feels:
Its wings are almost free—its home, its harbour
    found,
Measuring the gulf, it stoops, and dares the final
    bound.

Oh, dreadful is the check—intense the agony—
When the ear begins to hear, and the eye begins to
    see;
When the pulse begins to throb, the brain to think
    again,
The soul to feel the flesh, and the flesh to feel the
    chain.

Yet I would lose no sting, would wish no torture less,
 The more that anguish racks, the earlier it will bless;
And robed in fires of hell, or bright with heavenly
    shine,
If it but herald death, the vision is divine!

Emily Brontë (1818–1848)

Eros

The sense of the world is short,—
Long and various the report,—
  To love and be beloved;
Men and gods have not outlearned it;
And, how oft soe'er they've turned it,
  'Tis not to be improved.

Ralph Waldo Emerson (1803–1882)

Friendship

A ruddy drop of manly blood
The surging sea outweighs,
The world uncertain comes and goes,
The lover rooted stays.
I fancied he was fled,—
And, after many a year,
Glowed unexhausted kindliness,
Like daily sunrise there.
My careful heart was free again,
O friend, my bosom said,
Through thee alone the sky is arched,
Through thee the rose is red;
All things through thee take nobler form,
And look beyond the earth,
The mill-round of our fate appears
A sun-path in thy worth.
Me too thy nobleness has taught
To master my despair;
The fountains of my hidden life
Are through thy friendship fair.

Ralph Waldo Emerson (1803–1882)

from In Memoriam

VII

Dark house, by which once more I stand
  Here in the long unlovely street,
  Doors, where my heart was used to beat
So quickly, waiting for a hand,

A hand that can be claspt no more—
  Behold me, for I cannot sleep,
  And like a guilty thing I creep
At earliest morning to the door.

He is not here; but far away
  The noise of life begins again,
  And ghastly thro' the drizzling rain
On the bald street breaks the blank day.

XIII

Tears of the widower, when he sees
  A late-lost form that sleep reveals,
  And moves his doubtful arms, and feels
Her place is empty, fall like these;

Which weep a loss for ever new,
  A void where heart on heart reposed;
  And, where warm hands have prest and closed,
Silence, till I be silent too;

Which weep the comrade of my choice,
    An awful thought, a life removed,
    The human-hearted man I loved,
A spirit, not a breathing voice.

L

Be near me when my light is low,
    When the blood creeps, and the nerves prick
    And tingle; and the heart is sick,
And all the wheels of being slow.

Be near me when the sensuous frame
    Is rack'd with pangs that conquer trust;
    And Time a maniac scattering dust,
And Life a Fury slinging flame.

Be near me when my faith is dry,
    And men the flies of latter spring,
    That lay their eggs, and sting and sing
And weave their petty cells and die.

Be near me when I fade away,
    To point the term of human strife,
    And on the low dark verge of life
The twilight of eternal day.

LX

He past; a soul of nobler tone:
    My spirit loved and loves him yet,
    Like some poor girl whose heart is set
On one whose rank exceeds her own.

He mixing with his proper sphere,
    She finds the baseness of her lot,
    Half jealous of she knows not what,
And envying all that meet him there.

XCIII

I shall not see thee. Dare I say
    No spirit ever brake the band
    That stays him from the native land
Where first he walk'd when claspt in clay?

No visual shade of some one lost,
    But he, the Spirit himself, may come
    Where all the nerve of sense is numb;
Spirit to Spirit, Ghost to Ghost.

O, therefore from thy sightless range
    With gods in unconjectured bliss,
    O, from the distance of the abyss
Of tenfold-complicated change,

Descend, and touch, and enter; hear
    The wish too strong for words to name;
    That in this blindness of the frame
My Ghost may feel that thine is near.

CXXIX

Dear friend, far off, my lost desire,
    So far, so near in woe and weal;
    O loved the most, when most I feel
There is a lower and a higher;

Known and unknown; human, divine;
  Sweet human hand and lips and eye;
  Dear heavenly friend that canst not die,
Mine, mine, for ever, ever mine;

Strange friend, past, present, and to be;
  Loved deeplier, darklier understood;
  Behold, I dream a dream of good,
And mingle all the world with thee.

Alfred, Lord Tennyson (1809–1892)

from I Sing the Body Electric

I sing the body electric,
The armies of those I love engirth me and I engirth
them,
They will not let me off till I go with them, respond
to them,
And discorrupt them, and charge them full with the
charge of the soul.

Was it doubted that those who corrupt their own
bodies conceal themselves?
And if those who defile the living are as bad as they
who defile the dead?
And if the body does not do fully as much as the
soul?
And if the body were not the soul, what is the soul?

2

The love of the body of man or woman balks account,
the body itself balks account,
That of the male is perfect, and that of the female is
perfect.

The expression of the face balks account,
But the expression of a well-made man appears not
only in his face,
It is in his limbs and joints also, it is curiously in the
joints of his hips and wrists,
It is in his walk, the carriage of his neck, the flex of
his waist and knees, dress does not hide him,

The strong sweet quality he has strikes through the
    cotton and broadcloth,
To see him pass conveys as much as the best poem,
    perhaps more,
You linger to see his back, and the back of his neck
    and shoulder-side.

The sprawl and fulness of babes, the bosoms and
    heads of women, the folds of their dress, their
    style as we pass in the street, the contour of their
    shape downwards,
The swimmer naked in the swimming-bath, seen as
    he swims through the transparent green-shine, or
    lies with his face up and rolls silently to and fro
    in the heave of the water,
The bending forward and backward of rowers in
    row-boats, the horseman in his saddle,
Girls, mothers, house-keepers, in all their
    performances,
The group of laborers seated at noon-time with
    their open dinner-kettles, and their wives
    waiting,
The female soothing a child, the farmer's daughter in
    the garden or cow-yard,
The young fellow hoeing corn, the sleigh-driver
    driving his six horses through the crowd,
The wrestle of wrestlers, two apprentice-boys, quite
    grown, lusty, good-natured, native-born, out on
    the vacant lot at sundown after work,
The coats and caps thrown down, the embrace of love
    and resistance,
The upper-hold and under-hold, the hair rumpled
    over and blinding the eyes;

The march of firemen in their own costumes, the play
      of masculine muscle through clean-setting
      trowsers and waist-straps,
The slow return from the fire, the pause when the bell
      strikes suddenly again, and the listening on the
      alert,
The natural, perfect, varied attitudes, the bent head,
      the curv'd neck and the counting;
Such-like I love—I loosen myself, pass freely, am at
      the mother's breast with the little child,
Swim with the swimmers, wrestle with wrestlers,
      march in line with the firemen, and pause, listen,
      count.

3

I knew a man, a common farmer, the father of five
      sons,
And in them the fathers of sons, and in them the
      fathers of sons.
This man was of wonderful vigor, calmness, beauty of
      person,
The shape of his head, the pale yellow and white of his
      hair and beard, the immeasurable meaning of his
      black eyes, the richness and breadth of his manners,
These I used to go and visit him to see, he was wise
      also,
He was six feet tall, he was over eighty years old, his
      sons were massive, clean, bearded, tan-faced,
      handsome,
They and his daughters loved him, all who saw him
      loved him,
They did not love him by allowance, they loved him
      with personal love,

He drank water only, the blood show'd like scarlet
      through the clear-brown skin of his face,
He was a frequent gunner and fisher, he sail'd his
      boat himself, he had a fine one presented to him
      by a ship-joiner, he had fowling-pieces presented
      to him by men that loved him,
When he went with his five sons and many grand-sons
      to hunt or fish, you would pick him out as the
      most beautiful and vigorous of the gang,
You would wish long and long to be with him, you
      would wish to sit by him in the boat that you and
      he might touch each other.

4

I have perceiv'd that to be with those I like is enough,
To stop in company with the rest at evening is enough,
To be surrounded by beautiful, curious, breathing,
      laughing flesh is enough,
To pass among them or touch any one, or rest my
      arm ever so lightly round his or her neck for a
      moment, what is this then?
I do not ask any more delight, I swim in it as in a sea.

There is something in staying close to men and
      women and looking on them, and in the contact
      and odor of them, that pleases the soul well,
All things please the soul, but these please the soul well.
[...]

9

O my body! I dare not desert the likes of you in other
      men and women, nor the likes of the parts of
      you,

I believe the likes of you are to stand or fall with the
    likes of the soul, (and that they are the soul,)
I believe the likes of you shall stand or fall with my
    poems, and that they are my poems,
Man's, woman's, child's, youth's, wife's, husband's,
    mother's, father's, young man's, young woman's
    poems,
Head, neck, hair, ears, drop and tympan of the ears,
Eyes, eye-fringes, iris of the eye, eyebrows, and the
    waking or sleeping of the lids,
Mouth, tongue, lips, teeth, roof of the mouth, jaws,
    and the jaw-hinges,
Nose, nostrils of the nose, and the partition,
Cheeks, temples, forehead, chin, throat, back of the
    neck, neck-slue,
Strong shoulders, manly beard, scapula, hind-
    shoulders, and the ample side-round of the chest,
Upper-arm, armpit, elbow-socket, lower-arm,
    arm-sinews, arm-bones,
Wrist and wrist-joints, hand, palm, knuckles, thumb,
    forefinger, finger-joints, finger-nails,
Broad breast-front, curling hair of the breast,
    breast-bone, breast-side,
Ribs, belly, backbone, joints of the backbone,
Hips, hip-sockets, hip-strength, inward and outward
    round, man-balls, man-root,
Strong set of thighs, well carrying the trunk above,
Leg-fibres, knee, knee-pan, upper-leg, under-leg,
Ankles, instep, foot-ball, toes, toe-joints, the heel;
All attitudes, all the shapeliness, all the belongings of
    my or your body or of any one's body, male or
    female,
The lung-sponges, the stomach-sac, the bowels sweet
    and clean,

The brain in its folds inside the skull-frame,
Sympathies, heart-valves, palate-valves, sexuality, maternity,
Womanhood, and all that is a woman, and the man that comes from woman,
The womb, the teats, nipples, breast-milk, tears, laughter, weeping, love-looks, love-perturbations and risings,
The voice, articulation, language, whispering, shouting aloud,
Food, drink, pulse, digestion, sweat, sleep, walking, swimming,
Poise on the hips, leaping, reclining, embracing, arm-curving and tightening,
The continual changes of the flex of the mouth, and around the eyes,
The skin, the sunburnt shade, freckles, hair,
The curious sympathy one feels when feeling with the hand the naked meat of the body,
The circling rivers the breath, and breathing it in and out,
The beauty of the waist, and thence of the hips, and thence downward toward the knees,
The thin red jellies within you or within me, the bones and the marrow in the bones,
The exquisite realization of health;
O I say these are not the parts and poems of the body only, but of the soul,
O I say now these are the soul!

Walt Whitman (1819–1892)

When I Heard at the Close of Day

When I heard at the close of the day how my name
    had been receiv'd with plaudits in the capitol, still
    it was not a happy night for me that follow'd,
And else when I carous'd, or when my plans were
    accomplish'd, still I was not happy,
But the day when I rose at dawn from the bed of
    perfect health, refresh'd, singing, inhaling the ripe
    breath of autumn,
When I saw the full moon in the west grow pale and
    disappear in the morning light,
When I wander'd alone over the beach, and
    undressing bathed, laughing with the cool waters,
    and saw the sun rise,
And when I thought how my dear friend my lover was
    on his way coming, O then I was happy,
O then each breath tasted sweeter, and all that day
    my food nourish'd me more, and the beautiful
    day pass'd well,
And the next came with equal joy, and with the next
    at evening came my friend,
And that night, while all was still I heard the waters
    roll slowly continually up the shores,
I heard the hissing rustle of the liquid and sands as
    directed to me whispering to congratulate me,
For the one I love most lay sleeping by me under the
    same cover in the cool night,

In the stillness in the autumn moonbeams his face
    was inclined toward me,
And his arm lay lightly around my breast—and that
    night I was happy.

               Walt Whitman (1819–1892)

We Two Boys Together Clinging

We two boys together clinging,
One the other never leaving,
Up and down the roads going, North and South
excursions making,
Power enjoying, elbows stretching, fingers clutching,
Arm'd and fearless, eating, drinking, sleeping, loving,
No law less than ourselves owning, sailing, soldiering,
thieving, threatening,
Misers, menials, priests alarming, air breathing, water
drinking, on the turf or the sea-beach dancing,
Cities wrenching, ease scorning, statutes mocking,
feebleness chasing,
Fulfilling our foray.

Walt Whitman (1819–1892)

A Retrospect

From this fair point of present bliss,
　　Where we together stand,
Let me look back once more, and trace
　　That long and desert land,
Wherein till now was cast my lot, and I could live,
　　　and thou wert not.

Strange that my heart could beat, and know
　　Alternate joy and pain,
That suns could roll from east to west,
　　And clouds could pass in rain,
And the slow hours without thee fleet, nor stay their
　　　noiseless silver feet.

What had I then? a Hope, that grew
　　Each hour more bright and dear,
The flush upon the eastern skies
　　That showed the sun was near:—
Now night has faded far away, my sun has risen,
　　　and it is day.

A dim Ideal of tender grace
　　In my soul reigned supreme;
Too noble and too sweet I thought
　　To live, save in a dream—
Within thy heart to-day it lies, and looks on me
　　　from thy dear eyes.

Some gentle spirit,—Love I thought,—
　　Built many a shrine of pain;

Though each false Idol fell to dust
    The worship was not vain,
But a faint radiant shadow cast back from our
        Love upon the Past.

And Grief, too, held her vigil there;
    With unrelenting sway
Breaking my cloudy visions down,
    Throwing my flowers away:—
I owe to her fond care alone that I may now be
        all thine own.

Fair Joy was there—her fluttering wings
    At times she strove to raise;
Watching through long and patient nights,
    Listening long eager days:
I know now that her heart and mine were waiting.
        Love, to welcome thine.

Thus I can read thy name throughout,
    And, now her task is done,
Can see that even that faded Past
    Was thine, belovèd one,
And so rejoice my Life may be all consecrated, dear,
        to thee.

Adelaide Proctor (1825–1864)

from Goblin Market

Morning and evening
Maids heard the goblins cry:
"Come buy our orchard fruits,
Come buy, come buy:
Apples and quinces,
Lemons and oranges,
Plump unpecked cherries,
Melons and raspberries,
Bloom-down-cheeked peaches,
Swart-headed mulberries,
Wild free-born cranberries,
Crab-apples, dewberries,
Pine-apples, blackberries,
Apricots, strawberries;—
All ripe together
In summer weather,—
Morns that pass by,
Fair eves that fly;
Come buy, come buy."
[...]
Evening by evening
Among the brookside rushes,
Laura bowed her head to hear,
Lizzie veiled her blushes:
Crouching close together
In the cooling weather,
With clasping arms and cautioning lips,
With tingling cheeks and finger tips.
"Lie close," Laura said,
Pricking up her golden head:
"We must not look at goblin men,

We must not buy their fruits:
Who knows upon what soil they fed
Their hungry thirsty roots?"
"Come buy," call the goblins
Hobbling down the glen.
"Oh," cried Lizzie, "Laura, Laura,
You should not peep at goblin men."
[...]
Curious Laura chose to linger
Wondering at each merchant man.
One had a cat's face,
One whisked a tail,
One tramped at a rat's pace,
One crawled like a snail,
One like a wombat prowled obtuse and furry,
One like a ratel tumbled hurry skurry.
She heard a voice like voice of doves
Cooing all together.
[...]
Laura stared but did not stir,
Longed but had no money:
The whisk-tailed merchant bade her taste
In tones as smooth as honey.
[...]
But sweet-tooth Laura spoke in haste:
"Good folk, I have no coin;
To take were to purloin:
I have no copper in my purse,
I have no silver either,
And all my gold is on the furze
That shakes in windy weather
Above the rusty heather."
"You have much gold upon your head,"
They answered all together:

"Buy from us with a golden curl."
She clipped a precious golden lock,
She dropped a tear more rare than pearl,
Then sucked their fruit globes fair or red:
Sweeter than honey from the rock,
Stronger than man-rejoicing wine,
Clearer than water flowed that juice;
She never tasted such before,
How should it cloy with length of use?
She sucked and sucked and sucked the more
Fruits which that unknown orchard bore;
She sucked until her lips were sore;
Then flung the emptied rinds away
But gathered up one kernel stone,
And knew not was it night or day
As she turned home alone.

Lizzie met her at the gate
Full of wise upbraidings:
"Dear, you should not stay so late,
Twilight is not good for maidens;
Should not loiter in the glen
In the haunts of goblin men.
Do you not remember Jeanie,
How she met them in the moonlight,
Took their gifts both choice and many,
Ate their fruits and wore their flowers
Plucked from bowers
Where summer ripens at all hours?
But ever in the noonlight
She pined and pined away;
Sought them by night and day,
Found them no more but dwindled and grew grey;
Then fell with the first snow,

63

While to this day no grass will grow
Where she lies low:
I planted daisies there a year ago
That never blow.
You should not loiter so."
"Nay, hush," said Laura:
"Nay, hush, my sister:
I ate and ate my fill,
Yet my mouth waters still;
To-morrow night I will
Buy more;" and kissed her.
[...]
Golden head by golden head,
Like two pigeons in one nest
Folded in each other's wings,
They lay down in their curtained bed:
Like two blossoms on one stem,
Like two flakes of new-fall'n snow,
Like two wands of ivory
Tipped with gold for awful kings.
Moon and stars gazed in at them,
Wind sang to them lullaby,
Lumbering owls forbore to fly,
Not a bat flapped to and fro
Round their rest:
Cheek to cheek and breast to breast
Locked together in one nest.
[...]
Day after day, night after night,
Laura kept watch in vain
In sullen silence of exceeding pain.
She never caught again the goblin cry:
"Come buy, come buy;"—
She never spied the goblin men

Hawking their fruits along the glen:
But when the noon waxed bright
Her hair grew thin and grey;
She dwindled, as the fair full moon doth turn
To swift decay and burn
Her fire away.
[...]
Till Laura dwindling
Seemed knocking at Death's door:
Then Lizzie weighed no more
Better and worse;
But put a silver penny in her purse,
Kissed Laura, crossed the heath with clumps
    of furze
At twilight, halted by the brook:
And for the first time in her life
Began to listen and look.

Laughed every goblin
When they spied her peeping:
[...]
"Look at our apples
Russet and dun,
Bob at our cherries,
Bite at our peaches,
Citrons and dates,
Grapes for the asking,
Pears red with basking
Out in the sun,
Plums on their twigs;
Pluck them and suck them,
Pomegranates, figs."—

"Good folk," said Lizzie,
Mindful of Jeanie:
"Give me much and many:"—
Held out her apron,
Tossed them her penny.
"Nay, take a seat with us,
Honour and eat with us,"
They answered grinning:
"Our feast is but beginning."
[...]
"Thank you," said Lizzie: "But one waits
At home alone for me:
So without further parleying,
If you will not sell me any
Of your fruits though much and many,
Give me back my silver penny
I tossed you for a fee."—
They began to scratch their pates,
No longer wagging, purring,
But visibly demurring,
Grunting and snarling.
One called her proud,
Cross-grained, uncivil;
Their tones waxed loud,
Their looks were evil.
Lashing their tails
They trod and hustled her,
Elbowed and jostled her,
Clawed with their nails,
Barking, mewing, hissing, mocking,
Tore her gown and soiled her stocking,
Twitched her hair out by the roots,
Stamped upon her tender feet,
Held her hands and squeezed their fruits

Against her mouth to make her eat.
[...]
One may lead a horse to water,
Twenty cannot make him drink.
Though the goblins cuffed and caught her,
Coaxed and fought her,
Bullied and besought her,
Scratched her, pinched her black as ink,
Kicked and knocked her,
Mauled and mocked her,
Lizzie uttered not a word;
Would not open lip from lip
Lest they should cram a mouthful in:
But laughed in heart to feel the drip
Of juice that syrupped all her face,
And lodged in dimples of her chin,
And streaked her neck which quaked like curd.
At last the evil people
Worn out by her resistance
Flung back her penny, kicked their fruit
Along whichever road they took,
Not leaving root or stone or shoot;
Some writhed into the ground,
Some dived into the brook
With ring and ripple,
Some scudded on the gale without a sound,
Some vanished in the distance.

In a smart, ache, tingle,
Lizzie went her way;
Knew not was it night or day;
Sprang up the bank, tore thro' the furze;
Threaded copse and dingle,
And heard her penny jingle

Bouncing in her purse,—
Its bounce was music to her ear.
She ran and ran
As if she feared some goblin man
Dogged her with gibe or curse
Or something worse:
But not one goblin skurried after,
Nor was she pricked by fear;
The kind heart made her windy-paced
That urged her home quite out of breath with haste
And inward laughter.

She cried "Laura," up the garden,
"Did you miss me?
Come and kiss me.
Never mind my bruises,
Hug me, kiss me, suck my juices
Squeezed from goblin fruits for you,
Goblin pulp and goblin dew.
Eat me, drink me, love me;
Laura, make much of me:
For your sake I have braved the glen
And had to do with goblin merchant men."
Laura started from her chair,
Flung her arms up in the air,
Clutched her hair:
"Lizzie, Lizzie, have you tasted
For my sake the fruit forbidden?
Must your light like mine be hidden,
Your young life like mine be wasted,
Undone in mine undoing
And ruined in my ruin,
Thirsty, cankered, goblin-ridden?"—
She clung about her sister,

Kissed and kissed and kissed her:
Tears once again
Refreshed her shrunken eyes,
Dropping like rain
After long sultry drouth;
Shaking with aguish fear, and pain,
She kissed and kissed her with a hungry mouth.
[...]
Life out of death.
That night long Lizzie watched by her,
Counted her pulse's flagging stir,
Felt for her breath,
Held water to her lips, and cooled her face
With tears and fanning leaves:
But when the first birds chirped about their eaves,
And early reapers plodded to the place
Of golden sheaves,
And dew-wet grass
Bowed in the morning winds so brisk to pass,
And new buds with new day
Opened of cup-like lilies on the stream,
Laura awoke as from a dream,
Laughed in the innocent old way,
Hugged Lizzie but not twice or thrice;
Her gleaming locks showed not one thread of grey,
Her breath was sweet as May
And light danced in her eyes.

Days, weeks, months, years
Afterwards, when both were wives
With children of their own;
Their mother-hearts beset with fears,
Their lives bound up in tender lives;
Laura would call the little ones

And tell them of her early prime,
Those pleasant days long gone
Of not-returning time:
Would talk about the haunted glen,
The wicked, quaint fruit-merchant men,
Their fruits like honey to the throat
But poison in the blood;
(Men sell not such in any town):
Would tell them how her sister stood
In deadly peril to do her good,
And win the fiery antidote:
Then joining hands to little hands
Would bid them cling together,
"For there is no friend like a sister
In calm or stormy weather;
To cheer one on the tedious way,
To fetch one if one goes astray,
To lift one if one totters down,
To strengthen whilst one stands."

Christina Rossetti (1830–1894)

My Secret

I tell my secret? No indeed, not I:
Perhaps some day, who knows?
But not to-day; it froze, and blows, and snows,
And you're too curious: fie!
You want to hear it? well:
Only, my secret's mine, and I won't tell.

Or, after all, perhaps there's none:
Suppose there is no secret after all,
But only just my fun.
To-day's a nipping day, a biting day;
In which one wants a shawl,
A veil, a cloak, and other wraps:
I cannot ope to every one who taps,
And let the draughts come whistling through my hall;
Come bounding and surrounding me,
Come buffeting, astounding me,
Nipping and clipping through my wraps and all.
I wear my mask for warmth: who ever shows
His nose to Russian snows
To be pecked at by every wind that blows?
You would not peck? I thank you for good will,
Believe, but leave that truth untested still.

Spring's an expansive time: yet I don't trust
March with its peck of dust,
Nor April with its rainbow-crowned brief showers,
Nor even May, whose flowers
One frost may wither through the sunless hours.

Perhaps some languid summer day,
When drowsy birds sing less and less,
And golden fruit is ripening to excess,
If there's not too much sun nor too much cloud,
And the warm wind is neither still nor loud,
Perhaps my secret I may say,
Or you may guess.

Christina Rossetti (1830–1894)

Come slowly, Eden

Come slowly, Eden!
Lips unused to thee,
Bashful, sip thy jasmines,
As the fainting bee,

Reaching late his flower,
Round her chamber hums,
Counts his nectars—enters,
And is lost in balms!

Emily Dickinson (1830–1886)

Wild Nights

Wild nights! Wild nights!
Were I with thee,
Wild nights should be
Our luxury!

Futile the winds
To a heart in port,—
Done with the compass,
Done with the chart.

Rowing in Eden!
Ah! the sea!
Might I but moor
To-night in thee!

Emily Dickinson (1830–1886)

With a Flower

I hide myself within my flower,
That wearing on your breast,
You, unsuspecting, wear me too—
And angels know the rest.

I hide myself within my flower,
That, fading from your vase,
You, unsuspecting, feel for me
Almost a loneliness.

Emily Dickinson (1830–1886)

Emancipation

No rack can torture me,
My soul's at liberty
Behind this mortal bone
There knits a bolder one

You cannot prick with saw,
Nor rend with scymitar.
Two bodies therefore be;
Bind one, and one will flee.

The eagle of his nest
No easier divest
And gain the sky,
Than mayest thou,

Except thyself may be
Thine enemy;
Captivity is consciousness,
So's liberty.

Emily Dickinson (1830–1886)

Her breast is fit for pearls

Her breast is fit for pearls,
But I was not a diver.
Her brow is fit for thrones,
But I had not a crest.
Her heart is fit for rest—
I, a sparrow, build there
Sweet of twigs and twine,
My perennial nest.

Emily Dickinson (1830–1886)

FIN DE SIÈCLE

from Dolores (Notre-Dame
des Sept Douleurs)

Cold eyelids that hide like a jewel
   Hard eyes that grow soft for an hour;
The heavy white limbs, and the cruel
   Red mouth like a venomous flower;
When these are gone by with their glories,
   What shall rest of thee then, what remain,
O mystic and sombre Dolores,
   Our Lady of Pain?
[...]
O lips full of lust and of laughter,
   Curled snakes that are fed from my breast,
Bite hard, lest remembrance come after
   And press with new lips where you pressed.
For my heart too springs up at the pressure,
   Mine eyelids too moisten and burn;
Ah, feed me and fill me with pleasure,
   Ere pain come in turn.
[...]
There are sins it may be to discover,
   There are deeds it may be to delight.
What new work wilt thou find for thy lover,
   What new passions for daytime or night?
What spells that they know not a word of
   Whose lives are as leaves overblown?
What tortures undreamt of, unheard of,
   Unwritten, unknown?

Algernon Swinburne (1837–1909)

Hymn

These things shall be, – a loftier race
   Than ere the world hath known shall rise
With flame of freedom in their souls,
   And light of knowledge in their eyes.

They shall be gentle, brave, and strong
   To spill no drop of blood, but dare
All that may plant man's lordship firm
   On earth and fire, and sea, and air.

Nation with nation, land with land,
   Unarmed shall live as comrades free;
In every heart and brain shall throb
   The pulse of one fraternity.

Man shall love man, with heart as pure
   And fervent as the young-eyed throng
Who chant their heavenly psalms before
   God's face with undiscordant song.

New arts shall bloom of loftier mould
   And mightier music fill the skies,
And every life shall be a song,
   When all the earth is paradise.

John Addington Symonds (1840–1893)

Apologia

Is it thy will that I should wax and wane,
    Barter my cloth of gold for hodden grey,
And at thy pleasure weave that web of pain
    Whose brightest threads are each a wasted day?

Is it thy will—Love that I love so well—
    That my Soul's House should be a tortured spot
Wherein, like evil paramours, must dwell
    The quenchless flame, the worm that dieth not?

Nay, if it be thy will I shall endure,
    And sell ambition at the common mart,
And let dull failure be my vestiture,
    And sorrow dig its grave within my heart.

Perchance it may be better so—at least
    I have not made my heart a heart of stone,
Nor starved my boyhood of its goodly feast,
    Nor walked where Beauty is a thing unknown.

Many a man hath done so; sought to fence
    In straitened bonds the soul that should be free,
Trodden the dusty road of common sense,
    While all the forest sang of liberty,

Not marking how the spotted hawk in flight
    Passed on wide pinion through the lofty air,
To where the steep untrodden mountain height
    Caught the last tresses of the Sun God's hair.

Or how the little flower he trod upon,
　The daisy, that white-feathered shield of gold,
Followed with wistful eyes the wandering sun
　Content if once its leaves were aureoled.

But surely it is something to have been
　The best belovèd for a little while,
To have walked hand in hand with Love, and seen
　His purple wings flit once across thy smile.

Ay! though the gorgèd asp of passion feed
　On my boy's heart, yet have I burst the bars,
Stood face to face with Beauty, known indeed
　The Love which moves the Sun and all the stars!

Oscar Wilde (1854–1900)

In the Forest

Out of the mid-wood's twilight
Into the meadow's dawn,
Ivory limbed and brown-eyed,
Flashes my Faun!

He skips through the copses singing,
And his shadow dances along,
And I know not which I should follow,
Shadow or song!

O Hunter, snare me his shadow!
O Nightingale, catch me his strain!
Else moonstruck with music and madness
I track him in vain!

Oscar Wilde (1854–1900)

Quia Multum Amavi

Dear Heart I think the young impassioned priest
    When first he takes from out the hidden shrine
His God imprisoned in the Eucharist,
    And eats the bread, and drinks the dreadful wine,

Feels not such awful wonder as I felt
    When first my smitten eyes beat full on thee,
And all night long before thy feet I knelt
    Till thou wert wearied of Idolatry.

Ah! had'st thou liked me less and loved me more,
    Through all those summer days of joy and rain,
I had not now been sorrow's heritor,
    Or stood a lackey in the House of Pain.

Yet, though remorse, youth's white-faced seneschal
    Tread on my heels with all his retinue,
I am most glad I loved thee—think of all
    The suns that go to make one speedwell blue!

Oscar Wilde (1854–1900)

Les Silhouettes

The sea is flecked with bars of grey
The dull dead wind is out of tune,
And like a withered leaf the moon
Is blown across the stormy bay.

Etched clear upon the pallid sand
The black boat lies: a sailor boy
Clambers aboard in careless joy
With laughing face and gleaming hand.

And overhead the curlews cry,
Where through the dusky upland grass
The young brown-throated reapers pass,
Like silhouettes against the sky.

Oscar Wilde (1854–1900)

To a Stranger

O faithful eyes, day after day as I see and know
    you—unswerving faithful and beautiful—going
    about your ordinary work unnoticed,
    I have noticed—I do not forget you.
    I know the truth the tenderness the courage, I know
the longings hidden quiet there.
    Go right on. Have good faith yet—keep that your
unseen treasure untainted.
    Many shall bless you. To many yet, though no word
    be spoken, your face shall shine as a lamp.
    It shall be remembered, and that which you have
    desired—in silence—shall come abundantly to
    you.

Edward Carpenter (1844–1929)

Summer Heat

Sun burning down on back and loins, penetrating the
    skin, bathing their flanks in sweat,
Where they lie naked on the warm ground, and the
    ferns arch over them,
Out in the woods, and the sweet scent of fir-needles
Blends with the fragrant nearness of their bodies;

In-armed together, murmuring, talking,
Drunk with wine of Eros' lips,
Hourlong, while the great wind rushes in the
    branches,
And the blue above lies deep beyond the fern-fronds
    and fir-tips;

Till, with the midday sun, fierce scorching, smiting,
Up from their woodland lair they leap, and smite,
And strike with wands, and wrestle, and bruise each
    other,
In savage play and amorous despite.

Edward Carpenter (1844–1929)

In the Deep Cave of the Heart

In the deep cave of the heart, far down,
   Running under the outward shows of the world and
     of people,
   Running under geographies, continents, under the
     fields and the roots of the grasses and trees,
     under the little thoughts and dreams of men, and
     the history of races,
   Deep, far down,
   I see feel and hear wondrous and divine things.
   Voices and faces are there; arms of lovers, known
     and unknown, reach forward and fold me;
   Words float, and fragrance of Time ascends, and
     Life ever circling.

Edward Carpenter (1844–1929)

Defiance

O make me thine before the longing dies,
That leaves me loverless and not thy friend,
Past this hour who shall such another send?
Before the gate be shut of paradise,
O let us walk there amorous and wise.
Remember we are love's, to bruise or bend:
And what thy words began let thy lips end,
I care not surely for the after sighs.

Stern and relentless be thy love to-day,
Harsher the pressure of thy hand on mine,
To-morrow judge us. We can wait, I say,
And at the verdict I shall not repine.
This mouth was made for love and meant for moans:
If that be guilty, why, much pain atones.

Marc-André Raffalovich (1864–1934)

In the Mile End Road

How like her! But 'tis she herself,
  Comes up the crowded street,
How little did I think, the morn,
  My only love to meet!

Whose else that motion and that mien?
  Whose else that airy tread?
For one strange moment I forgot
  My only love was dead.

Amy Levy (1861–1889)

To Lallie

Up those Museum steps you came,
And straightway all my blood was flame,
                    O Lallie, Lallie!

The world (I had been feeling low)
In one short moment's space did grow
                    A happy valley.

There was a friend, my friend, with you;
A meagre dame, in peacock blue
                    Apparelled quaintly:

This poet-heart went pit-a-pat;
I bowed and smiled and raised my hat;
                    You nodded—faintly.

My heart was full as full could be;
You had not got a word for me,
                    Not one short greeting;

That nonchalant small nod you gave
(The tyrant's motion to the slave)
                    Sole mark'd our meeting.

Is it so long? Do you forget
That first and last time that we met?
                    The time was summer;

93

The trees were green; the sky was blue;
Our host presented me to you—
    A tardy comer.

You look'd demure, but when you spoke
You made a little, funny joke,
    Yet half pathetic.

Your gown was grey, I recollect,
I think you patronized the sect
    They call "æsthetic."

I brought you strawberries and cream,
I plied you long about a stream
    With duckweed laden;

We solemnly discussed the—heat.
I found you shy and very sweet,
    A rosebud maiden.

Ah me, to-day! You passed inside
To where the marble gods abide:
    Hermes, Apollo,

Sweet Aphrodite, Pan; and where,
For aye reclined, a headless fair
    Beats all fairs hollow.

And I, I went upon my way,
Well—rather sadder, let us say;
    The world looked flatter.

I had been sad enough before,
A little less, a little more,
What *does* it matter?

Amy Levy (1861–1889)

At a Dinner Party

With fruit and flowers the board is deckt,
  The wine and laughter flow;
I'll not complain—could one expect
  So dull a world to know?

You look across the fruit and flowers,
  My glance your glances find.—
It is our secret, only ours,
  Since all the world is blind.

Amy Levy (1861–1889)

The Mystic's Vision

I

Ah! I shall kill myself with dreams!
  These dreams that softly lap me round
Through trance-like hours, in which, meseems,
  That I am swallowed up and drowned;
Drowned in your love which flows o'er me
As o'er the seaweed flows the sea.

II

In watches of the middle night,
  'Twixt vesper and 'twixt matin bell,
With rigid arms and straining sight,
  I wait within my narrow cell;
With muttered prayers, suspended will,
I wait your advent—statue-still.

III

Across the Convent garden walls
  The wind blows from the silver seas;
Black shadow of the cypress falls
  Between the moon-meshed olive trees;
Sleep-walking from their golden bowers,
Flit disembodied orange flowers.

IV

And in God's consecrated house,
  All motionless from head to feet,
My heart awaits her heavenly Spouse,
  As white I lie on my white sheet;

With body lulled and soul awake,
I watch in anguish for your sake.

V

And suddenly, across the gloom,
   The naked moonlight sharply swings;
A Presence stirs within the room,
   A breath of flowers and hovering wings:
Your Presence without form and void,
Beyond all earthly joys enjoyed.

VI

My heart is hushed, my tongue is mute,
   My life is centred in your will;
You play upon me like a lute
   Which answers to its master's skill,
Till passionately vibrating,
Each nerve becomes a throbbing string.

VII

Oh, incommunicably sweet!
   No longer aching and apart,
As rain upon the tender wheat,
   You pour upon my thirsty heart;
As scent is bound up in the rose,
Your love within my bosom glows.

VIII

Unseen, untouched, unheard, unknown,
   You take possession of your bride;
I lose myself to live alone
   In you, who once were crucified

For me, that now would die in you,
As in the sun a drop of dew.

IX

Fish may not perish in the deep,
 Nor sparrows fall through yielding air,
Pure gold in hottest flame will keep;
 How should I fail and falter where
You are, O Lord, in whose control
For ever lies my living soul?

X

Ay, break through every wall of sense,
 And pierce my flesh as nails did pierce
Your bleeding limbs in anguish tense,
 And torture me with bliss so fierce,
That self dies out, as die it must,
Ashes to ashes, dust to dust.

XI

Thus let me die, so loved and lost,
 Annihilated in my dreams!
Nor force me, an unwilling ghost,
 To face the loud day's brutal beams;
The noisy world's inanities,
All vanity of vanities.

Mathilde Blind (1841–1896)

It was deep April

It was deep April, and the morn
  Shakspere was born;
The world was on us, pressing sore;
My Love and I took hands and swore,
  Against the world, to be
Poets and lovers evermore,
To laugh and dream on Lethe's shore,
To sing to Charon in his boat,
Heartening the timid souls afloat;
Of judgment never to take heed,
But to those fast-locked souls to speed,
Who never from Apollo fled,
Who spent no hour among the dead;
  Continually
  With them to dwell,
Indifferent to heaven and hell.

*'Michael Field' (Katherine Bradley 1846–1914
            and Edith Cooper 1862–1913)*

Unbosoming

The love that breeds
In my heart for thee!
As the iris is full, brimful of seeds,
And all that it flowered for among the reeds
Is packed in a thousand vermilion-beads
That push, and riot, and squeeze, and clip,
Till they burst the sides of the silver scrip,
And at last we see
What the bloom, with its tremulous, bowery fold
Of zephyr-petal at heart did hold:
So my breast is rent
With the burthen and strain of its great content;
For the summer of fragrance and sighs is dead,
The harvest-secret is burning red,
And I would give thee, after my kind,
The final issues of heart and mind.

'Michael Field' (*Katherine Bradley 1846–1914
and Edith Cooper 1862–1913*)

The Sleeping Venus

GIORGIONE

The Dresden Gallery

Here is Venus by our homes
And resting on the verdant swell
Of a soft country flanked with mountain domes:
She has left her archèd shell,
Has left the barren wave that foams,
Amid earth's fruitful tilths to dwell.
   Nobly lighted while she sleeps
   As sward-lands or the corn-field sweeps,
   Pure as are the things that man
   Needs for life and using can
   Never violate nor spot—
   Thus she slumbers in no grot,
    But on open ground,
    With the great hill-sides around.

And her body has the curves,
The same extensive smoothness seen
In yonder breadths of pasture, in the swerves
Of the grassy mountain-green
That for her propping pillow serves:
There is a sympathy between
   Her and Earth of largest reach,
   For the sex that forms them each
   Is a bond, a holiness,
   That unconsciously must bless
   And unite them, as they lie
   Shameless underneath the sky

A long, opal cloud
Doth in noontide haze enshroud.

O'er her head her right arm bends;
And from the elbow raised aloft
Down to the crossing knees a line descends
Unimpeachable and soft
As the adjacent slope that ends
In chequered plain of hedge and croft.
　　Circular as lovely knolls,
　　Up to which a landscape rolls
　　With desirous sway, each breast
　　Rises from the level chest,
　　One in contour, one in round—
　　Either exquisite, low mound
　　Firm in shape and given
　　To the August warmth of heaven.

With bold freedom of incline,
With an uttermost repose,
From hip to herbage-cushioned foot the line
Of her left leg stretching shows
Against the turf direct and fine,
Dissimilar in grace to those
　　Little bays that in and out
　　By the ankle wind about;
　　Or that shallow bend, the right
　　Curled-up knee has brought to sight
　　Underneath its bossy rise,
　　Where the loveliest shadow lies!
　　Charmèd umbrage rests
　　On her neck and by her breasts.

Her left arm remains beside
The plastic body's lower heaves,
Controlled by them, as when a river-side
With its sandy margin weaves
Deflections in a lenient tide;
Her hand the thigh's tense surface leaves,
    Falling inward. Not even sleep
    Dare invalidate the deep,
    Universal pleasure sex
    Must unto itself annex—
    Even the stillest sleep; at peace,
    More profound with rest's increase,
    She enjoys the good
    Of delicious womanhood.

Cheek and eyebrow touch the fold
Of the raised arm that frames her hair,
Her braided hair in colour like to old
Copper glinting here and there:
While through her skin of olive-gold
The scarce carnations mount and share
    Faultlessly the oval space
    Of her temperate, grave face.
    Eyelids underneath the day
    Wrinkle as full buds that stay,
    Through the tranquil, summer hours,
    Closed although they might be flowers;
    The red lips shut in
    Gracious secrets that begin.

On white drapery she sleeps,
That fold by fold is stained with shade;
Her mantle's ruddy pomegranate in heaps
For a cushion she has laid

Beneath her; and the glow that steeps
Its grain of richer depth is made
　By an overswelling bank,
　Tufted with dun grasses rank.
　From this hillock's outer heaves
　One small bush defines its leaves
　Broadly on the sober blue
　The pale cloud-bank rises to,
　Whilst it sinks in bland
　Sunshine on the distant land.

Near her resting-place are spread,
In deep or greener-lighted brown,
Wolds, that half-withered by the heat o'erhead,
Press up to a little town
Of castle, archway, roof and shed,
Then slope in grave continuance down:
　On their border, in a group,
　Trees of brooding foliage droop
　Sidelong; and a single tree
　Springs with bright simplicity,
　Central from the sunlit plain.
　Of a blue no flowers attain,
　On the fair, vague sky
　Adamantine summits lie.

And her resting is so strong
That while we gaze it seems as though
She had lain thus the solemn glebes among
In the ages far ago
And would continue, till the long,
Last evening of Earth's summer glow
　In communion with the sweet
　Life that ripens at her feet:

We can never fear that she
From Italian fields will flee,
For she does not come from far,
She is of the things that are;
And she will not pass
While the sun strikes on the grass.

*'Michael Field' (Katherine Bradley 1846–1914
and Edith Cooper 1862–1913)*

Two Loves

I dreamed I stood upon a little hill,
And at my feet there lay a ground, that seemed
Like a waste garden, flowering at its will
With buds and blossoms. There were pools that
    dreamed
Black and unruffled; there were white lilies
A few, and crocuses, and violets
Purple or pale, snake-like fritillaries
Scarce seen for the rank grass, and through green nets
Blue eyes of shy peryenche winked in the sun.
And there were curious flowers, before unknown,
Flowers that were stained with moonlight, or with
    shades
Of Nature's willful moods; and here a one
That had drunk in the transitory tone
Of one brief moment in a sunset; blades
Of grass that in an hundred springs had been
Slowly but exquisitely nurtured by the stars,
And watered with the scented dew long cupped
In lilies, that for rays of sun had seen
Only God's glory, for never a sunrise mars
The luminous air of Heaven. Beyond, abrupt,
A grey stone wall, o'ergrown with velvet moss
Uprose; and gazing I stood long, all mazed
To see a place so strange, so sweet, so fair.
And as I stood and marvelled, lo! across
The garden came a youth; one hand he raised
To shield him from the sun, his wind-tossed hair
Was twined with flowers, and in his hand he bore
A purple bunch of bursting grapes, his eyes
Were clear as crystal, naked all was he,

White as the snow on pathless mountains frore,
Red were his lips as red wine-spilith that dyes
A marble floor, his brow chalcedony.
And he came near me, with his lips uncurled
And kind, and caught my hand and kissed my mouth,
And gave me grapes to eat, and said, 'Sweet friend,
Come I will show thee shadows of the world
And images of life. See from the South
Comes the pale pageant that hath never an end.'
And lo! within the garden of my dream
I saw two walking on a shining plain
Of golden light. The one did joyous seem
And fair and blooming, and a sweet refrain
Came from his lips; he sang of pretty maids
And joyous love of comely girl and boy,
His eyes were bright, and 'mid the dancing blades
Of golden grass his feet did trip for joy;
And in his hand he held an ivory lute
With strings of gold that were as maidens' hair,
And sang with voice as tuneful as a flute,
And round his neck three chains of roses were.
But he that was his comrade walked aside;
He was full sad and sweet, and his large eyes
Were strange with wondrous brightness, staring wide
With gazing; and he sighed with many sighs
That moved me, and his cheeks were wan and white
Like pallid lilies, and his lips were red
Like poppies, and his hands he clenched tight,
And yet again unclenched, and his head
Was wreathed with moon-flowers pale as lips of death.
A purple robe he wore, o'erwrought in gold
With the device of a great snake, whose breath
Was fiery flame: which when I did behold
I fell a-weeping, and I cried, 'Sweet youth,

Tell me why, sad and sighing, thou dost rove
These pleasant realms? I pray thee speak me sooth
What is thy name?' He said, 'My name is Love.'
Then straight the first did turn himself to me
And cried, 'He lieth, for his name is Shame,
But I am Love, and I was wont to be
Alone in this fair garden, till he came
Unasked by night; I am true Love, I fill
The hearts of boy and girl with mutual flame.'
Then sighing, said the other, 'Have thy will,
I am the love that dare not speak its name.'

Lord Alfred Douglas (1870–1945)

In Praise of Shame

Last night unto my bed methought there came
Our lady of strange dreams, and from an urn
She poured live fire, so that mine eyes did burn
At the sight of it. Anon the floating flame
Took many shapes, and one cried: "I am Shame
That walks with Love, I am most wise to turn
Cold lips and limbs to fire; therefore discern
And see my loveliness, and praise my name."

And afterwards, in radiant garments dressed
With sound of flutes and laughing of glad lips,
A pomp of all the passions passed along
All the night through; till the white phantom ships
Of dawn sailed in. Whereat I said this song,
"Of all sweet passions Shame is the loveliest."

Lord Alfred Douglas (1870–1945)

Impression de Nuit

London.

See what a mass of gems the city wears
Upon her broad live bosom! row on row
Rubies and emeralds and amethysts glow.
See! that huge circle like a necklace, stares
With thousands of bold eyes to heaven, and dares
The golden stars to dim the lamps below,
And in the mirror of the mire I know
The moon has left her image unawares.

That's the great town at night: I see her breasts,
Pricked out with lamps they stand like huge black
    towers.
I think they move! I hear her panting breath.
And that's her head where the tiara rests.
And in her brain, through lanes as dark as death,
Men creep like thoughts ... The lamps are like pale
    flowers.

Lord Alfred Douglas (1870–1945)

The Dead Poet

I dreamed of him last night, I saw his face
All radiant and unshadowed of distress,
And as of old, in music measureless,
I heard his golden voice and marked him trace
Under the common thing the hidden grace,
And conjure wonder out of emptiness,
Till mean things put on beauty like a dress
And all the world was an enchanted place.

And then methought outside a fast locked gate
I mourned the loss of unrecorded words,
Forgotten tales and mysteries half said,
Wonders that might have been articulate,
And voiceless thoughts like murdered singing birds.
And so I woke and knew that he was dead.

Lord Alfred Douglas (1870–1945)

Marriage

No more alone sleeping, no more alone waking,
  Thy dreams divided, thy prayers in twain;
Thy merry sisters tonight forsaking,
  Never shall we see, maiden, again.

Never shall we see thee, thine eyes glancing,
  Flashing with laughter and wild in glee,
Under the mistletoe kissing and dancing,
  Wantonly free.

There shall come a matron walking sedately,
  Low-voiced, gentle, wise in reply.
Tell me, O tell me, can I love her greatly?
  All for her sake must the maiden die!

Mary Coleridge (1861–1907)

The White Women

Where dwell the lovely, wild white women folk,
   Mortal to man?
They never bowed their necks beneath the yoke,
They dwelt alone when the first morning broke
   And Time began.

Taller are they than man, and very fair,
   Their cheeks are pale,
At sight of them the tiger in his lair,
The falcon hanging in the azure air,
   The eagles quail.

The deadly shafts their nervous hands let fly
   Are stronger than our strongest—in their form
Larger, more beauteous, carved amazingly,
And when they fight, the wild white women cry
   The war-cry of the storm.

Their words are not as ours. If man might go
   Among the waves of Ocean when they break
And hear them—hear the language of the snow
Falling on torrents—he might also know
   The tongue they speak.

Pure are they as the light; they never sinned,
   But when the rays of the eternal fire
Kindle the West, their tresses they unbind
And fling their girdles to the Western wind,
   Swept by desire.

Lo, maidens to the maidens then are born,
   Strong children of the maidens and the breeze,
Dreams are not—in the glory of the morn,
Seen through the gates of ivory and horn—
   More fair than these.

And none may find their dwelling. In the shade
   Primeval of the forest oaks they hide.
One of our race, lost in an awful glade,
Saw with his human eyes a wild white maid,
   And gazing, died.

Mary Coleridge (1861–1907)

EARLY TWENTIETH CENTURY

from A Shropshire Lad

The street sounds to the soldiers' tread,
    And out we troop to see:
A single redcoat turns his head,
    He turns and looks at me.

My man, from sky to sky's so far,
    We never crossed before;
Such leagues apart the world's ends are,
    We're like to meet no more;

What thoughts at heart have you and I
    We cannot stop to tell;
But dead or living, drunk or dry,
    Soldier, I wish you well.

A. E. Housman (1859–1936)

The laws of God, the laws of man

The laws of God, the laws of man,
He may keep that will and can;
Not I: let God and man decree
Laws for themselves and not for me;
And if my ways are not as theirs
Let them mind their own affairs.
Their deeds I judge and much condemn,
Yet when did I make laws for them?
Please yourselves, say I, and they
Need only look the other way.
But no, they will not; they must still
Wrest their neighbour to their will,
And make me dance as they desire
With jail and gallows and hell-fire
And how am I to face the odds
Of man's bedevilment and God's?
I, a stranger and afraid
In a world I never made.
They will be master, right or wrong;
Though both are foolish, both are strong.
And since, my soul, we cannot fly
To Saturn nor to Mercury,
Keep we must, if keep we can,
These foreign laws of God and man.

A. E. Housman (1859–1936)

Oh who is that young sinner

Oh who is that young sinner with the handcuffs on his
    wrists?
And what has he been after that they groan and shake
    their fists?
And wherefore is he wearing such a conscience-
    stricken air?
Oh they're taking him to prison for the colour of his
    hair.

'Tis a shame to human nature, such a head of hair as
    his;
In the good old time 'twas hanging for the colour that
    it is;
Though hanging isn't bad enough and flaying would
    be fair
For the nameless and abominable colour of his hair.

Oh a deal of pains he's taken and a pretty price he's
    paid
To hide his poll or dye it of a mentionable shade;
But they've pulled the beggar's hat off for the world to
    see and stare,
And they're haling him to justice for the colour of his
    hair.

Now 'tis oakum for his fingers and the treadmill for
    his feet

And the quarry-gang on Portland in the cold and in
    the heat,
And between his spells of labour in the time he has to
    spare
He can curse the God that made him for the colour
    of his hair.

A. E. Housman (1859–1936)

Reminiscences

Just once we met,
It seems so long ago,
So long . . . and yet
Men would not think it so
Who count their time by years.
Just once we met,
And now we never meet,
Is it regret
(I lost a friend so sweet)
That stings my heart to tears?

I clasped your hand,
But scarcely said a word;
We stood as children stand
Whose souls are stirred
To great shy love they cannot comprehend.
I clasped your hand
And looked into your eyes;
My spirit spanned
Your spirit's mysteries,
But feared to call you "friend."

Olive Cunstance (1874–1944)

Gifts

Come near! you are my friend and I will wear
Gems for your sake, and flowers in my hair;
Garments of silver gauze, and cloth of gold ...
And I will give you power to have and hold,
And passion, and delight and ecstasy.
What will you give to me?

And I will give you, if you will but stay,
The magic mirror of the dawn, where day
Waking, beholds the wonder of her face—
If you will keep me yet in your embrace,
And let me dream of Love's eternity.
What will you give to me?

Yes! I will give you the gold veils of light,
And the dark spangled curtains of the night ...
And I will give you as a flower unfurled,
The proud and marvellous beauty of the world,
And all the wild, white horses of the sea.
What will you give to me? ...

Olive Cunstance (1874–1944)

St. Sebastian

So beautiful in all thine agony!
So radiant in thine infinite despair . . .
Oh, delicate mouth, brave eyes, and curled bright
    hair . . .
Oh, lovely body lashed to the rough tree:
What brutal fools were those that gave to thee
Red roses of thine outraged blood to wear,
Laughed at thy bitter pain and loathed the fair
Bruised flower of thy victorious purity?

Marvellous Beauty . . . target of the world,
How all Love's arrows seek thy joy, Oh Sweet!
And wound the white perfection of thy youth!
How all the poisoned spears of hate are hurled
Against thy sorrow when thou darest to meet
With martyrdom men's mockery of the truth!

Olive Cunstance (1874–1944)

Asphodel

As some pale shade in glorious battle slain,
  On beds of rue, beside the silent streams,
  Recalls outworn delights in happy dreams;
The play of oars upon the flashing main,
The speed of runners, and the swelling vein,
  And toil in pleasant upland field that teems
  With vine and gadding gourd—until he seems
To feel wan memories of the sun again
  And scent the vineyard slopes when dawn is wet,
But feels no ache within his loosened knees
  To join the runners where the course is set,
Nor smite the billows of the fruitless seas,—
  So I recall our day of passion yet,
  With sighs and tenderness, but no regret.

Willa Cather (1873–1947)

On Entering into a Closer Friendship

How will it feel to live so close to you,
  In daily contact for a little space,
   To watch each changing thought upon your face,
Each passing mood, each gesture fond and new?

Dear, I am half afraid to enter through
  This open portal, to that holy place
   That lies beyond, lest I should fail in grace
Whose love is blind, because it is so true.

Give me your hand, that I may find my way
  About the garden of your mind, and see
   With inward eyes all that was hid from me
Before I knew you as I do to-day;

And seeing, fall and worship, aye, and pray
  For greater understanding. Timidly
   I crave admittance to your life, and free
Sweet intercourse, and leave to love—and stay.

Radclyffe Hall (1880–1943)

To Italy

O Italy of chiming bells,
Of pilgrim shrines and holy wells,
Of incense mist and secret prayers,
Profound and sweet as scented airs
Blown from a field of lily flowers!

O Italy of pagan vine,
That thrills with sap of sun-born wine,
Drenching the Christian soul with red
Warm liquid of a faith long dead,
Wafting it back to sensuous hours.

No mortal woman ever held
Such sweet inconstancies, or welled
With such hot springs of turbid fire;
No being throbbed with such desire,
Thy very air is ecstacy!

O pagan goddess, from whose lips
The gentle Christian worship slips,
I fear thee, knowing what thou art
Yet I adore thee; take my heart
I am thy lover, Italy!

Radclyffe Hall (1880–1943)

The Beginning

Some day I shall rise and leave my friends
And seek you again through the world's far ends,
You whom I found so fair,
(Touch of your hands and smell of your hair!),
My only god in the days that were.
My eager feet shall find you again,
Though the sullen years and the mark of pain
Have changed you wholly; for I shall know
(How could I forget having loved you so?),
In the sad half-light of evening,
The face that was all my sunrising.
So then at the ends of the earth I'll stand
And hold you fiercely by either hand,
And seeing your age and ashen hair
I'll curse the thing that once you were,
Because it is changed and pale and old
(Lips that were scarlet, hair that was gold!),
And I loved you before you were old and wise,
When the flame of youth was strong in your eyes,
　—And my heart is sick with memories.

Rupert Brooke (1887–1915)

Success

I think if you had loved me when I wanted;
   If I'd looked up one day, and seen your eyes,
And found my wild sick blasphemous prayer granted,
   And your brown face, that's full of pity and wise,
Flushed suddenly; the white godhead in new fear
   Intolerably so struggling, and so shamed;
Most holy and far, if you'd come all too near,
   If earth had seen Earth's lordliest wild limbs tamed,
Shaken, and trapped, and shivering, for *my* touch—
   Myself should I have slain? or that foul you?
But this the strange gods, who had given so much,
   To have seen and known you, this they might not
     do.
One last shame's spared me, one black word's
     unspoken;
And I'm alone; and you have not awoken.

Rupert Brooke (1887–1915)

130

The Way That Lovers Use

The way that lovers use is this;
  They bow, catch hands, with never a word,
And their lips meet, and they do kiss,
  —So I have heard.

They queerly find some healing so,
  And strange attainment in the touch;
There is a secret lovers know,
  —I have read as much.

And theirs no longer joy nor smart,
  Changing or ending, night or day;
But mouth to mouth, and heart on heart,
  —So lovers say.

Rupert Brooke (1887–1915)

Together

I wonder if you really send
  These dreams of you that come and go!
I like to say, "She thought of me,
  And I have known it." Is it so?

Though other friends are by your side,
  Yet sometimes it must surely be
They wonder where your thoughts have gone—
  Because I have you here with me.

And when the busy day is done,
  When work is ended, voices cease,
And everyone has said good-night
  In fading twilight, then, in peace,

Idly I rest; you come to me,
  Your dear love holds me close to you.
If I could see you face to face,
  It would not be more sweet and true.

And now across the weary miles
  Light from my star shines. Is it, dear,
You never really went away—
  I said farewell, and—kept you here?

Sarah Orne Jewett (1849–1909)

Harry Ploughman

Hard as hurdle arms, with a broth of goldish flue
Breathed round; the rack of ribs; the scooped flank;
   lank
Rope-over thigh; knee-nave; and barrelled shank—
   Head and foot, shoulder and shank—
By a grey eye's heed steered well, one crew, fall to;
Stand at stress. Each limb's barrowy brawn, his thew
That onewhere curded, onewhere sucked or sank—
   Soared or sank—,
Though as a beechbole firm, finds his, as at a roll-call,
   rank
And features, in flesh, what deed he each must do—
   His sinew-service where do.

He leans to it, Harry bends, look. Back, elbow, and
   liquid waist
In him, all quail to the wallowing o' the plough: 's
   cheek crimsons; curls
Wag or crossbridle, in a wind lifted, windlaced—
   See his wind- lilylocks -laced;
Churlsgrace, too, child of Amansstrength, how it
   hangs or hurls
Them—broad in bluff hide his frowning feet lashed!
   raced
With, along them, cragiron under and cold furls—
   With-a-fountain's shining-shot furls.

Gerard Manley Hopkins (1844–1889)

Glimpse

I saw you fooling often in the tents
With fair dishevelled hair and laughing lips,
And frolic elf lights in your careless eyes,
As who had never known the taste of tears
Or the world's sorrow. Then on march one night,
Halted beneath the stars I heard the sound
Of talk and laughter, and glanced back to see
If you were there. But you stood far apart
And silent, bowed upon your rifle butt,
And gazed into the night as one who sees.
I marked the drooping lips and fathomless eyes
And knew you brooded on immortal things.

W. N. Hodgson (1893–1916)

The Dead Soldier

Thy dear brown eyes which were as depths where
    truth
  Lay bowered with frolic joy, but yesterday
Shone with the fire of thy so guileless youth,
  Now ruthless death has dimmed and closed for aye.

Those sweet red lips, that never knew the stain
  Of angry words or harsh, or thoughts unclean,
Have sung their last gay song. Never again
  Shall I the harvest of their laughter glean.

The goodly harvest of thy laughing mouth
  Is garnered in; and lo! the golden grain
Of all thy generous thoughts, which knew no drouth
  Of meanness, and thy tender words remain

Stored in my heart; and though I may not see
  Thy peerless form nor hear thy voice again,
The memory lives of what thou wast to me.
  We knew great love . . . We have not lived in vain.

Sydney Oswald (1880–1926)

Lament in 1915

I call you, and I call you. Oh come home,
You lonely creature. Curse the foreign clown
Who plugged you with that lead, and knocked you
    down.
Stand up again and laugh, you wandering friend;
Say, as you would: "It's just a little hole;
It will soon mend."
Walk now into the room. Come! Come! Come!
    Come!

Come! we will laugh together all the night.
(We shall have poured ourselves a glass or two.)
Sit down. Our mutual mirth will reach its height
When we remember how they called you dead,
And I shall ask you how it felt, and you—
"Oh, nothing. Just a tumble. Rather hot,
The feeling in my side; and then my head
A trifle dizzy, but I'm back again.
I lay out there too long, and I've still got,
When I think of it, just a little pain."

I know the way you tumbled . . . Once you slid
And landed on your side. I noticed then
A trick of falling; some peculiar glide—
A curious movement, not like other men.
But did your mouth drop open? Did your breath
Hurt you? What sort of feeling quickly came,
When you discovered that it might be death?

And what will happen if I shout your name?
Perhaps you may be there behind the door,

And if I raise my voice a little more,
You'll swing it open. I don't know how thick
The black partition is between us two.
Answer, if you can hear me; friend, be quick . . .
Listen, the door-bell rang! Perhaps it's you.

You're in the room. You're sitting in that chair.
You are! . . . I will go down. It *was* the bell.
You *may* be waiting at the door as well.

Am I not certain I shall find you there? . . .

You're rigged in your best uniform to-day;
You take a momentary martial stand,
Then step inside and hold me out your hand,
And laugh in that old solitary way.

You don't know why you did it. All this while
You've slaved and sweated. Now you're very strong,
And so you tell me with a knowing smile:
"We're going out to Flanders before long."
I thought you would come back with an ugly hole
Below your thigh,
And ask for sympathy and wander lame;
I thought you'd be that same
Grumbling companion without self-control—
I never thought you'd die.

*

Now let us both forget this brief affair:
Let us begin our friendship all again.
I'm going down to meet you on the stair.
Walk to me! Come! for I can see you plain.
How strange! A moment I did think you dead.

How foolish of me!
Friend! friend! Are you dumb?
Why are you pale? Why do you hang your head?
You see me? Here's my hand. Why don't you come?
Don't make me angry. You are there, I know.
Is not my house your house? There is a bed
Upstairs. You're tired. Lie down; you must come
   home.
Some men are killed . . . not you. Be as you were.
And yet—Somehow it's dark down all the stair.
I'm standing at the door. You are not there.

Harold Munro (1879–1932)

Strange Meeting

It seemed that out of the battle I escaped
Down some profound dull tunnel, long since scooped
Through granites which Titanic wars had groined.
Yet also there encumbered sleepers groaned,
Too fast in thought or death to be bestirred.
Then, as I probed them, one sprang up, and stared
With piteous recognition in fixed eyes,
Lifting distressful hands as if to bless.
And by his smile, I knew that sullen hall;
By his dead smile I knew we stood in Hell.
With a thousand fears that vision's face was grained;
Yet no blood reached there from the upper ground,
And no guns thumped, or down the flues made moan.
"Strange friend," I said, "Here is no cause to mourn."
"None," said the other, "Save the undone years,
The hopelessness. Whatever hope is yours,
Was my life also; I went hunting wild
After the wildest beauty in the world,
Which lies not calm in eyes, or braided hair,
But mocks the steady running of the hour,
And if it grieves, grieves richlier than here.
For by my glee might many men have laughed,
And of my weeping something has been left,
Which must die now. I mean the truth untold,
The pity of war, the pity war distilled.
Now men will go content with what we spoiled.
Or, discontent, boil bloody, and be spilled.
They will be swift with swiftness of the tigress,
None will break ranks, though nations trek from
        progress.
Courage was mine, and I had mystery;

Wisdom was mine, and I had mastery;
To miss the march of this retreating world
Into vain citadels that are not walled.
Then, when much blood had clogged their
    chariot-wheels
I would go up and wash them from sweet wells,
Even with truths that lie too deep for taint.
I would have poured my spirit without stint
But not through wounds; not on the cess of war.
Foreheads of men have bled where no wounds were.
I am the enemy you killed, my friend.
I knew you in this dark; for so you frowned
Yesterday through me as you jabbed and killed.
I parried; but my hands were loath and cold.
Let us sleep now . . ."

Wilfred Owen (1893–1918)

To Eros

In that I loved you, Love, I worshipped you;
In that I worshipped well, I sacrificed.
All of most worth I bound and burnt and slew:
The innocent small things, fair friends and Christ.

I slew all falser loves, I slew all true,
For truth is the prime lie men tell a boy.
Glory I cast away, as bridegrooms do
Their splendid garments in their haste of joy.

But when I fell and held your sandalled feet,
You laughed; you loosed away my lips; you rose.
I heard the singing of your wings' retreat;
And watched you, far-flown, flush the Olympian
    snows,
Beyond my hoping. Starkly I returned
To stare upon the ash of all I burned.

Wilfred Owen (1893–1918)

How Do I Love Thee?

I cannot woo thee as the lion his mate,
With proud parade and fierce prestige of presence;
Nor thy fleet fancy may I captivate
With pastoral attitudes in flowery pleasance;
Nor will I kneeling court thee with sedate
And comfortable plans of husbandhood;
Nor file before thee as a candidate ...
I cannot woo thee as a lover would.

To wrest thy hand from rivals, iron-gloved,
Or cheat them by a craft, I am not clever.
But I do love thee even as Shakespeare loved,
Most gently wild, and desperately for ever,
Full-hearted, grave, and manfully in vain,
With thought, high pain, and ever vaster pain.

Wilfred Owen (1893–1918)

Peace

Peace flows into me
  As the tide to the pool by the shore;
  It is mine forevermore,
It will not ebb like the sea.

I am the pool of blue
  That worships the vivid sky;
  My hopes were heaven-high,
They are all fulfilled in you.

I am the pool of gold
  When sunset burns and dies—
  You are my deepening skies;
Give me your stars to hold.

Sara Teasdale (1884–1933)

Saturday Market

Bury your heart in some deep green hollow
   Or hide it up in a kind old tree
Better still, give it the swallow
   When she goes over the sea.

In Saturday Market there's eggs a 'plenty
   And dead-alive ducks with their legs tied down,
Grey old gaffers and boys of twenty—
   Girls and the women of the town—
Pitchers and sugar-sticks, ribbons and laces,
   Posies and whips and dicky-birds' seed,
Silver pieces and smiling faces,
   In Saturday Market they've all they need.

What were you showing in Saturday Market
   That set it grinning from end to end
Girls and gaffers and boys of twenty—?
   Cover it close with your shawl, my friend—
Hasten you home with the laugh behind you,
   Over the down—, out of sight,
Fasten your door, though no one will find you
   No one will look on a Market night.

See, you, the shawl is wet, take out from under
   The red dead thing—. In the white of the moon
On the flags does it stir again? Well, and no wonder!
   Best make an end of it; bury it soon.
If there is blood on the hearth who'll know it?
   Or blood on the stairs,
When a murder is over and done why show it?
   In Saturday Market nobody cares.

Then lie you straight on your bed for a short, short
    weeping
And still, for a long, long rest,
There's never a one in the town so sure of sleeping
  As you, in the house on the down with a hole in
    your breast.

Think no more of the swallow,
    Forget, you, the sea,
Never again remember the deep green hollow
    Or the top of the kind old tree!

Charlotte Mew (1869–1928)

Absence

Sometimes I know the way
You walk, up over the bay;
It is a wind from that far sea
That blows the fragrance of your hair to me.

Or in this garden when the breeze
Touches my trees
To stir their dreaming shadows on the grass
I see you pass.

In sheltered beds, the heart of every rose
Serenely sleeps to-night. As shut as those
Your guarded heart; as safe as they form the beat,
    beat
Of hooves that tread dropped roses in the street.

Turn never again
On these eyes blind with a wild rain
Your eyes; they were stars to me.—
There are things stars may not see.

But call, call, and though Christ stands
Still with scarred hands
Over my mouth, I must answer. So
I will come—He shall let me go!

Charlotte Mew (1869–1928)

The Call

From our low seat beside the fire
Where we have dozed and dreamed and watched the
    glow
Or raked the ashes, stopping so
We scarcely saw the sun or rain
Above, or looked much higher
Than this same quiet red or burned-out fire.
To-night we heard a call,
A rattle on the window-pane,
A voice on the sharp air,
And felt a breath stirring our hair,
A flame within us: Something swift and tall
Swept in and out and that was all.
Was it a bright or a dark angel? Who can know?
It left no mark upon the snow,
But suddenly it snapped the chain
Unbarred, flung wide the door
Which will not shut again;
And so we cannot sit here any more.
We must arise and go:
The world is cold without
And dark and hedged about
With mystery and enmity and doubt,
But we must go
Though yet we do not know
Who called, or what marks we shall leave upon the
    snow.

Charlotte Mew (1869–1928)

In a Garden

Gushing from the mouths of stone men
To spread at ease under the sky
In granite-lipped basins,
Where iris dabble their feet
And rustle to a passing wind,
The water fills the garden with its rushing,
In the midst of the quiet of close-clipped lawns.

Damp smell the ferns in tunnels of stone,
Where trickle and plash the fountains,
Marble fountains, yellowed with much water.

Splashing down moss-tarnished steps
It falls, the water;
And the air is throbbing with it.
With its gurgling and running.
With its leaping, and deep, cool murmur.

And I wished for night and you.
I wanted to see you in the swimming-pool,
White and shining in the silver-flecked water.
While the moon rode over the garden,
High in the arch of night,
And the scent of the lilacs was heavy with stillness.

Night, and the water, and you in your whiteness,
    bathing!

Amy Lowell (1874–1925)

A Decade

When you came, you were like red wine and honey,
And the taste of you burnt my mouth with its
    sweetness.
Now you are like morning bread,
Smooth and pleasant.
I hardly taste you at all for I know your savour,
But I am completely nourished.

Amy Lowell (1874–1925)

I love to see

I love to see
Her looking up at me,
Stretched on a bed
In her pink dressing gown,
Her arms above her head,
Her hair all down.
I love to see
Her smiling up at me.

Lesbia Harford (1891–1927)

I can't feel the sunshine

I can't feel the sunshine
Or see the stars aright
For thinking of her beauty
And her kisses bright.

She would let me kiss her
Once and not again.
Deeming soul essential,
Sense doth she disdain.

If I should once kiss her,
I would never rest
Till I had lain hour long
Pillowed on her breast.

Lying so, I'd tell her
Many a secret thing
God has whispered to me
When my soul took wing.

Would that I were Sappho,
Greece my land, not this!
There the noblest women,
When they loved, would kiss.

Lesbia Harford (1891–1927)

Episode of Hands

The unexpected interest made him flush.
Suddenly he seemed to forget the pain,—
Consented,—and held out
One finger from the others.

The gash was bleeding, and a shaft of sun
That glittered in and out among the wheels,
Fell lightly, warmly, down into the wound.

And as the fingers of the factory owner's son,
That knew a grip for books and tennis
As well as one for iron and leather,—
As his taut, spare fingers wound the gauze
Around the thick bed of the wound,
His own hands seemed to him
Like wings of butterflies
Flickering in sunlight over summer fields.

The knots and notches,—many in the wide
Deep hand that lay in his,—seemed beautiful.
They were like the marks of wild ponies' play,—
Bunches of new green breaking a hard turf.

And factory sounds and factory thoughts
Were banished from him by that larger, quieter hand
That lay in his with the sun upon it.
And as the bandage knot was tightened
The two men smiled into each other's eyes.

Hart Crane (1899–1932)

A Memory of June

When June comes dancing o'er the death of May,
   With scarlet roses tinting her green breast,
And mating thrushes ushering in her day,
   And Earth on tiptoe for her golden guest,

I always see the evening when we met—
   The first of June baptized in tender rain—
And walked home through the wide streets, gleaming
     wet,
   Arms locked, our warm flesh pulsing with love's
     pain.

I always see the cheerful little room,
   And in the corner, fresh and white, the bed,
Sweet scented with a delicate perfume,
   Wherein for one night only we were wed;

Where in the starlit stillness we lay mute,
   And heard the whispering showers all night long,
And your brown burning body was a lute
   Whereon my passion played his fevered song.

When June comes dancing o'er the death of May,
   With scarlet roses staining her fair feet,
My soul takes leave of me to sing all day
   A love so fugitive and so complete.

Claude McKay (1889–1948)

A Red Flower

Your lips are like a southern lily red,
  Wet with the soft rain-kisses of the night,
In which the brown bee buries deep its head,
  When still the dawn's a silver sea of light.

Your lips betray the secret of your soul,
  The dark delicious essence that is you,
A mystery of life, the flaming goal
  I seek through mazy pathways strange and new.

Your lips are the red symbol of a dream.
  What visions of warm lilies they impart,
That line the green bank of a fair blue stream,
  With butterflies and bees close to each heart!

Brown bees that murmur sounds of music rare,
  That softly fall upon the languorous breeze,
Wafting them gently on the quiet air
  Among untended avenues of trees.

O were I hovering, a bee, to probe
  Deep down within your scented heart, fair flower,
Enfolded by your soft vermilion robe,
  Amorous of sweets, for but one perfect hour!

Claude McKay (1889–1948)

After the Winter

Some day, when trees have shed their leaves
   And against the morning's white
The shivering birds beneath the eaves
   Have sheltered for the night,
We'll turn our faces southward, love,
   Toward the summer isle
Where bamboos spire to shafted grove
   And wide-mouthed orchids smile.

And we will seek the quiet hill
   Where towers the cotton tree,
And leaps the laughing crystal rill,
   And works the droning bee.
And we will build a cottage there
   Beside an open glade,
With black-ribbed blue-bells blowing near,
   And ferns that never fade.

Claude McKay (1889–1948)

Tavern

I'll keep a little tavern
  Below the high hill's crest,
Wherein all grey-eyed people
  May set them down and rest.

There shall be plates a-plenty,
  And mugs to melt the chill
Of all the grey-eyed people
  Who happen up the hill.

There sound will sleep the traveller,
  And dream his journey's end,
But I will rouse at midnight
  The falling fire to tend.

Aye, 'tis a curious fancy—
  But all the good I know
Was taught me out of two grey eyes
  A long time ago.

Edna St Vincent Millay (1892–1950)

The Little Ghost

I knew her for a little ghost
  That in my garden walked;
The wall is high—higher than most—
  And the green gate was locked.

And yet I did not think of that
  Till after she was gone—
I knew her by the broad white hat,
  All ruffled, she had on.

By the dear ruffles round her feet,
  By her small hands that hung
In their lace mitts, austere and sweet,
  Her gown's white folds among.

I watched to see if she would stay,
  What she would do—and oh!
She looked as if she liked the way
  I let my garden grow!

She bent above my favourite mint
  With conscious garden grace.
She smiled and smiled—there was no hint
  Of sadness in her face.

She held her gown on either side
  To let her slippers show,
And up the walk she went with pride,
  The way great ladies go.

And where the wall is built in new
  And is of ivy bare
She paused—then opened and passed through
  A gate that once was there.

Edna St Vincent Millay (1892–1950)

Ebb

I know what my heart is like
  Since your love died:
It is like a hollow ledge
Holding a little pool
  Left there by the tide,
  A little tepid pool,
Drying inward from the edge.

Edna St Vincent Millay (1892–1950)

Oh, think not I am faithful

Oh, think not I am faithful to a vow!
Faithless am I save to love's self alone.
Were you not lovely I would leave you now:
After the feet of beauty fly my own.
Were you not still my hunger's rarest food,
And water ever to my wildest thirst,
I would desert you–think not but I would!–
And seek another as I sought you first.
But you are mobile as the veering air,
And all your charms more changeful than the tide,
Wherefore to be inconstant is no care:
I have but to continue at your side.
So wanton, light and false, my love, are you,
I am most faithless when I most am true.

Edna St Vincent Millay (1892–1950)

Tableau

For Donald Duff

Locked arm in arm they cross the way,
  The black boy and the white,
The golden splendor of the day,
  The sable pride of night.

From lowered blinds the dark folk stare,
  And here the fair folk talk,
Indignant that these two should dare
  In unison to walk.

Oblivious to look and word
  They pass, and see no wonder
That lightning brilliant as a sword
  Should blaze the path of thunder.

Countee Cullen (1903–1946)

FURTHER DEVELOPMENTS

A Litany for Survival

For those of us who live at the shoreline
standing upon the constant edges of decision
crucial and alone
for those of us who cannot indulge
the passing dreams of choice
who love in doorways coming and going
in the hours between dawns
looking inward and outward
at once before and after
seeking a now that can breed
futures
like bread in our children's mouths
so their dreams will not reflect
the death of ours;

For those of us
who were imprinted with fear
like a faint line in the center of our foreheads
learning to be afraid with our mother's milk
for by this weapon
this illusion of some safety to be found
the heavy-footed hoped to silence us
For all of us
this instant and this triumph
We were never meant to survive.

And when the sun rises we are afraid
it might not remain
when the sun sets we are afraid
it might not rise in the morning
when our stomachs are full we are afraid

of indigestion
when our stomachs are empty we are afraid
we may never eat again
when we are loved we are afraid
love will vanish
when we are alone we are afraid
love will never return
and when we speak we are afraid
our words will not be heard
nor welcomed
but when we are silent
we are still afraid

So it is better to speak
remembering
we were never meant to survive.

Audre Lorde (1934–1992)

The Man with Night Sweats

I wake up cold, I who
Prospered through dreams of heat
Wake to their residue,
Sweat, and a clinging sheet.

My flesh was its own shield:
Where it was gashed, it healed.

I grew as I explored
The body I could trust
Even while I adored
The risk that made robust,

A world of wonders in
Each challenge to the skin.

I cannot but be sorry
The given shield was cracked,
My mind reduced to hurry,
My flesh reduced and wrecked.

I have to change the bed,
But catch myself instead

Stopped upright where I am
Hugging my body to me
As if to shield it from
The pains that will go through me,

As if hands were enough
To hold an avalanche off.

Thom Gunn (1929–2004)

Stonewall – A Poem

When there is a riot
is like
when there is a crisis
in a lot of lives.
It is when a hinge creaks,
when a hinge swings,
and things change.

The place
where there is a riot
where there is a crisis
That wasn't important
till it was important.
Important for what happened there.

Stonewall
Was just a bar
Where gay men
and some dykes
went to drink
Or to get laid.
It wasn't a bar
You went to
if you were
Too poor, too queer, too young, too brown.
It was a bar
Down the street.
One night

it was the place
where things changed.

2

You have to remember
you have to imagine
you have to feel

how things were,
back in the day.

Some nights you went to a bar
And your life changed
Not for the better.

The police would come in
Because no one had paid them
Or just 'cause they could.
And the police dragged you out

You stood in night court
Or lay in a cell
with drunks, hoods and thieves
who knew you were queer
so worse than they were
and no-one heard you scream.

The press took your name
And printed your name
And that changed your life.

You lost
Your job

Your home
The marriage where you hid,
Your children and your future and your hope.

And people went to bars
For all the reasons people go to bars
To drink, or to get laid.
And sometimes their lives changed.

That night
At the Stonewall bar
lives changed
and some for the better.

3

We don't know all their names
The people in the bar
when the police went in
And then things changed.

So make them up.

Harold was there
After the symphony,
Or after La Boheme –
He'd have to check.

He keeps his diaries still.
You don't call him Harry,
Or Harriet,
He's Harold. Still.

He went there
Because he wanted a drink
and wanted a fuck
and Judy had died
and he wanted a friend.

Arnie was there
He worked construction,
He wasn't queer –
He told himself.
He wanted a blow job
And not to have to pay.

And Harold spoke to Arnie
And Arnie had a beer
And Harold had a white wine
And then the police were there.

And Harold relaxed
And was sad about Judy
And dreaming of the man who got away
And Arnie thought well
I'm fucked
If this gets out.
On the construction site.
So Harold shouted fuck off pigs

And Arnie shoved a cop
And somebody hit Harold in the head
And Arnie said don't hit my friend
And then it all kicked off.

Or, it wasn't quite like that.
It was Betty

Who taught school
Out in the suburbs
And was talking to Dean
Who had an Elvis quiff
And could fix your bike better than any man.
And a cop told Betty he could fuck her better
And ran his fingers up and down her spine
And Dean said, fuck off pig
And then it all kicked off.

Or it was Baby Val
There for her birthday
She was just eighteen.
The first time she'd been out
Wholly in drag - and she just cried and cried
The pigs had ruined her birthday.
So she cried
And then it all kicked off.

4

And so the police, they dragged
Harold and Dean
And Betty and Arnie and the rest
Out of the bar and out into the street.

And then it all kicked off.

And they held Baby Val
Inside for questioning
And someone screamed
The pigs are beating Val in the back room
And then it all kicked off

173

The riot was the bar
And
The riot was the street.
The street where people lived
The street where people walked
Too young, too queer, too poor, too brown.

Looking for handouts
Or daddies for the night
Or cheap street drugs
In drag and out of it.

The people with nothing to lose.

I know their names
Because they are my kind

Marsha P. Johnson – Present
Allyson Allante – Present
Tammy Novak – Present
Zazu Nova – Present
Birdy Riveira – Present
Stormé DeLarverie – Present
Miss Major – Present
Holly Woodlawn – Present
Sylvia Rivera – Present – Probably
In spirit anyway
So print the legend –
Sylvia was there
And maybe threw
The bottlesmash we heard around the world

And all the rest
Drag queens and street queens and hair fairies and
    gender illusionists and Warhol superstars
Street Transvestite Action Radicals
– but that was later
– still they were all there

In jeans that looked like you could peel them off
like fruit skin
like peach skin
like grape skin
In eyeliner and eyelashes and paint
So thick it didn't crack
so thick it didn't run
tear gas made no impression on that slap.
And showgirl stockings

And their hair fluffed up.
Hurling dustbins
in high heels
screaming screaming screaming queens
We are the stonewall girls
We wear our hair in curls
We wear no underwear
We braid our pubic hair

And they were all so young
Sylvia was seventeen
Sweet seventeen
Allysson was fourteen
Parents threw trans kids away
So young back then
Marsha was twenty-five
The oldest lady on the street

And it kicked off
And Tammy ran away
Hid in Joe Tish's flat
But she'd been there

And it kicked off
And Holly got there late
In time to throw a brick
But she was there

They were the stonewall girls
They wore their hair in curls

They are my sisters, so I sing of them
Like Homer did dead heroes
And they're dead, the most of them.
Sylvia's liver went
When she was fifty
Marsha – she was found
face down and floating
in the Hudson.

Allyson's still here, married again,
and Holly, just about.
Sometimes trans folk make old bones.

The stonewall girls
Their hair in curls

Don't no-one ever say they were not there.

5

This much we know
That night everything changed
And they were there
All of them, they were there.

The ones I know because they are my kind
The ones I know because I made them up

They changed their lives
They changed all of our lives

The hinge creaked
When the door opened
The police came out of the bar

Into the street
And we came
Out of the closet
Into the street
Out of the closet
into the street.
Out of the closet
into the street.

Roz Kaveney (b. 1949)

Pride

There is pride in my bite.
Lipstick smudge on neck,
vampire teeth in,
are you afraid you will turn into me?

There is pride in the bashing,
bashing of my back.
Bash back, to face.
imagine fist into your jeer.

There is pride in the way I yell.
'Who you calling faggot?'
'What the fuck are you looking at?'
'Did you not know that us freaks have mouths?'

There is pride in my heels wandering.
Forceful, stomps on grounds
Pushes into knees that stop
Who knew fear could look this fierce?

There is pride in my flexibility.
To go from death drop
To dancing with death
It is your loss that you only hear my fingers click.

You tell me of pride in rainbows,
In flags and flat stomachs, muscles and chests,

Pride in our celebration,
In unity and glee,
And I spit out my pride in rebellion.
The pride in saying:
I am a freak, and you cannot fuck with me.

Travis Alabanza (b. 1995)

Index of poets

Index of titles

Index of first lines

Permissions Acknowledgements

'Stonewall – A Poem' first published in *Dialectic of the Flesh* (Midsummer Night Press), then in Roz's *Selected Poems 2009 – 2021* (Team Angelica).

'Pride' © Travis Alabanza. First published in the *Gay Times* and reproduced with permission of David Godwin Associates.